Safety and Risk in Primary School Physical Education

Physical education and sport in schools is undergoing renewed emphasis and the primary sector key stages are rightly seen as fundamental elements in the new initiatives.

The majority of primary school teachers are non-specialists and there is, therefore, a particular need for information on safe planning and practice in physical education to be designed to meet their specific requirements.

Safety is a central issue in PE and, as risk assessment is now a statutory part of Health and Safety at Work requirements, it is vitally important that all staff have a clear understanding of their responsibilities. As all schools are now obliged to undertake risk management, this book addresses a very real need.

Safety and Risk in Primary School Physical Education gives comprehensive coverage of all aspects of safety in PE in primary schools, including:

- The school's and teachers' legal responsibilities
- Policies on good practice and risk
- Pupil readiness
- Equipment and the Environment
- Each subject area included in the National Curriculum; Gymnastics, Games, Dance, Athletics, Adventure Activities and Swimming.
- Checklists of key points for safe practice

John Severs has spent many years working in primary schools. He was a class teacher and an LEA advisory teacher in primary school PE before working as a lecturer in teacher training with particular responsibility for professional PE. He currently works as a consultant to primary educators and as an expert witness.

Safety and Risk in Primary School Physical Education

A guide for teachers

John Severs

with Peter Whitlam and Jes Woodhouse

Routledge
Taylor & Francis Group

LONDON AND NEW YORK

First published 2003
by Routledge
11 New Fetter Lane, London EC4P 4EE

Simultaneously published in the USA and Canada
by Routledge
29 West 35th Street, New York, NY 10001

Routledge is an imprint of the Taylor & Francis Group

Typeset in Sabon by
HWA Text and Data Management Ltd, Tunbridge Wells

British Library Cataloguing in Publication Data
A catalogue record for this book is available from the British
Library

Library of Congress Cataloging in Publication Data
Severs, John, 1935–
    Safety and risk in primary school physical education: a guide for
teachers / John Severs with Peter Whitlam and Jes Woodhouse.
        p.   cm.
    1. Physical education and training – Study and teaching
(Elementary) – Great Britain.   2. Schools – Great Britain – Safety
measures.   I. Whitlam, Peter, 1949–   II. Woodhouse, Jes.
III. Title.

GV365.5.G7S48   2003
372.86´028´9–dc21   2002037128

ISBN 0–415–31815–7 (hbk)
ISBN 0–415–26879–6 (pbk)

Contents

Figures

Contributors

John Severs originally trained as a PE specialist and has worked as a junior school class teacher and an advisory teacher in primary school physical education. He has held a number of posts as a lecturer on ITT courses with responsibility for primary professional physical education training. He has tutored in-service courses for LEAs and other bodies and has written two books and many articles for journals on a range of primary physical education aspects including safety and the law. He is a trained expert witness and currently works as a consultant.

Peter Whitlam is General Secretary of the British Association of Advisors and Lecturers in Physical Education. Prior to this he worked in schools, higher education and advisory work with local education authorities. He is a trained legal expert, holds higher degrees in law and physical education, and has led in-service courses in many local authorities in the UK as well as abroad.

Jes Woodhouse is currently a lecturer in higher education with responsibility for primary school oriented ITT and in-service teacher training. He has been a teacher and advisory teacher of physical education, in each case with responsibility for outdoor and adventurous activities. He has led in-service courses on this area and written a number of articles on the subject for PE journals.

Foreword

This book seeks to provide relevant and much needed information on safe practice for those concerned with physical education in primary schools.

The subject has always demanded that safe practice be properly acknowledged and addressed, thereby promoting both the safety and safety education of young people. The importance, however, has increased with the growth of legislation in this area, particularly under the requirements for Health and Safety at Work and the incorporated risk management procedures.

Teachers need to be fully aware of the implications of the law and the duty of care responsibilities they bear. The content of this publication will greatly assist their awareness in this regard, helping them to develop as informed practitioners who are able to exercise sound judgement in their work.

Mr Severs has a long and successful background in physical education, as a teacher, local authority advisory teacher, lecturer, consultant and expert witness. He is a knowledgeable enthusiast whose wide experience in the field has enabled him to produce a timely publication.

The content will inform readers on suitable physical activities combined with safe practice for infant and junior school pupils, providing information and guidance by which students and teachers of the primary age group may engage in physical education with confidence and competence.

It should be available for reference in schools and Initial Teacher Training establishments as an essential complement to the programmes and schemes of the National Curriculum.

Norman R. Eve
Safety Officer, British Association of Advisers and
Lecturers in Physical Education (BAALPE)

Acknowledgements

My wife, Alice, for patient checking of the text.

Norman Eve for his encouragement and wise counsel.

Brian Scraton for the gymnastics apparatus artwork.

Head teacher, Allan Suthren, class teacher, Audrey Hughes, and children from Years 2 and 5 at Birtley East Primary School (Gateshead LEA) for the photographs.

The Football Association for permission to reprint Guidelines on Goalposts from the *Football Curriculum Guide* (see Appendix F).

The Amateur Swimming Association, British Association of Advisers and Lecturers in Physical Education, the English Schools Athletics Association and Mini-Basketball England for permission to quote from publications.

Those many representatives of different bodies who have talked to me in person or on the telephone or responded to my requests by letter.

Abbreviations

AOTTs	Adults Other Than Teachers
ASA	Amateur Swimming Association
BA	Bachelor of Arts
BAALPE	British Association of Advisers and Lecturers in Physical Education
BCU	British Canoe Union
BEd	Bachelor of Education
BSc	Bachelor of Science
BSI	British Standards Institution
CRB	Criminal Records Bureau
DfES	Department for Education and Skills (formerly DfEE)
DfEE	Department for Education and Employment
EAP	Emergency Action Plan
ECB	English Cricket Board
ESAA	English Schools Athletics Association
FA	Football Association
FE	Further Education
HSC	Heath and Safety Commission
HSE	Health and Safety Executive
HSW	Health and Safety at Work
ICT	Information and Communication Technology
ITT	Initial Teacher Training
KS	Key Stage
LEA	Local Education Authority
MHSWR	Management of Health and Safety at Work Regulations
NC	National Curriculum
NCF	National Coaching Foundation (now sports coach UK)
NGB	National Governing Body (i.e. of sports)
NOP	Normal Operating Plan
NQT	Newly Qualified Teacher
QCA	Qualifications and Curriculum Authority
PE	Physical Education
PEAUK	Physical Education Association of the United Kingdom
PGCE	Post-Graduate Certificate in Education
PSOP	Pool Safety Operating Procedure
RLSS	Royal Life-Saving Society
RYA	Royal Yachting Association
SEN	Special Educational Needs
STA	Swimming Teachers Association

Introduction

Safety and Risk in Primary school Physical Education is intended first and foremost as an easy to use but, nevertheless, comprehensive guide to both the 'background' and the 'chalk-face' factors which dictate whether curriculum and extra-curricular activities for Foundation and KS1 and 2 pupils can be considered safe.

It is a guide for head teachers in regard to school policies in PE, risk assessment and management, employment of Adults Other Than Teachers etc. and for curriculum leaders, but, above all, it is for the class teacher. It looks directly at pupil needs and constraints, planning, organisation, equipment, the transporting and setting up of apparatus, duties in respect of the law, preparation, progression and approach. It concentrates on what teachers need to know in regard to risk and the practical areas prescribed in the National Curriculum for children from these age groups. It is concerned with teaching, aiming not simply to identify the negative – what not to do – but to promote the positive in regard to good practice.

It is meant as a reference book and, also, a practical manual. It is seen as a valuable aid to planning schemes and lessons, to formulating school policy documents and as a basis for staff discussions and a text for professional courses in PE.

It is accepted that in physical education there will always be an element of risk. We do not wish to emasculate activities so that they are totally anodyne and present no challenge. This book is intended to help reduce risks to acceptable levels, to ensure that preventable accidents do not occur. It is intended not as a substitute for but as an aid to good professional judgement.

It is not judgemental. Activities such as relays, which some would question on educational grounds, are covered fully in recognition of the fact that they will be done in many schools. Only if activities or approaches or types of equipment are believed to be intrinsically dangerous, or may become so if done or used in a particular way, is it recommended that they are not included or used in PE programmes.

Some important aspects, such as risk, are covered in more than one chapter or section of a chapter so that they are read and understood in relation to a particular context or set of duties.

Health-Related Exercise is a statuory requirement at each key stage of the National Curriculum and along with warming up and cooling down and reference to safe and unsafe exercises is covered in an appendix.

Basic information, common to all or some of the practical areas, is covered in the 'background' chapters, 1 and, particularly, 2 and 3, and in those concentrating on risk, 4 and 5. Specific advice on subject aspects is given in chapters 6–12.

The views expressed are those of the authors. They do not necessarily reflect those of any organisations that they may be members of or associated with.

Photocopying

Much of the chapter contents could be usefully copied and given to teachers for use on an ongoing basis or in planning lessons. Some sections would be of value to coaches, instructors and others assisting with lessons. Where sections of a chapter are believed to be of vital importance and could usefully be copied for easy reference by all staff, they have been marked with the symbol ¤. This also applies to summaries of major points in a subject area presented in the form of a checklist or as golden rules.

1 The teacher and the law

This first chapter looks at

- legal requirements in respect of Duty of Care and the Health and Safety at Work Acts, particularly in respect of risk, liability, teacher qualifications, the employment of coaches and others to take or assist with curricular and extra-curricular activities, and trainee teachers;
- how to avoid charges of negligence, with particular emphasis on good practice.

Duty of care

Teachers, in common with all members of the public, have a duty to ensure that others are not harmed by their actions or their failure to act.

Through their training and experience, teachers are expected to have the necessary expertise and to know a great deal more about the actions and reactions of children in given school curricular and extra-curricular activities than other adults, including responsible parents. This is particularly so in physical education with its attendant risks and a *higher level of duty of care* is now expected of anyone teaching this subject.

Teachers will always retain responsibility for classes and groups of children regardless of who may be engaged in actually teaching the children and be responsible for the lesson content (e.g. a swimming instructor employed by the LEA or school, a coach at a local sports centre or a sports development officer).

Duty of care applies regardless of where the activity is taking place (e.g. on the school premises, local authority swimming pools or sports centres, parks or other school premises) or who is actually taking the lessons (see *Adults other than teachers* below).

Negligence

Negligence can only be proved if a pupil is injured as a result of taking part in an activity and it can be shown that the teacher was, in some way, responsible.

For example, it may be alleged that instructions were not clear, the pupil was asked to do something that was beyond his or her capabilities, the equipment used was faulty, or the supervision was not at the level that could reasonably be expected.

Liability

Normally, the teacher's employers would be responsible for the actions of the teacher while engaged in curricular and extra-curricular work and this should be clearly stated in the contract of employment. Any action by a claimant would be against the employer, who would be responsible for paying any damages and costs that may be awarded. This is called *vicarious liability*.

In the past, in respect of state schools, the employer would be the LEA. However, with the changes that have taken place in regard to the amount of control delegated to the school, the position is not always clear. It is very much worth checking to ensure that employers are responsible and that the teacher will not be held personally liable and expected to pay damages.

If it is shown that the teacher had acted in a totally irresponsible way, either by pursuing a particular course of action or by failing to take obvious precautions, the teacher may be held to be partially responsible for the action and asked to pay a proportion of the damages awarded. Fortunately, this is extremely rare.

If teachers take pupils to participate in activities outside the normal extra-curricular programme (e.g. a tournament held on a Sunday, a local club training session held in the evening or adventure activities held at a specialist centre), they should ensure that they have the approval of the head teacher and/or governors.

If activities, such as extra-curricular training, are deemed not to be covered by the head or governors, teachers would require additional insurance to cover possible liability arising from an accident. This may be personal, organised by the school or arranged by any club or organisation involved.

Teachers should check carefully to ensure that this additional insurance does provide the appropriate cover for the activity in question.

It should not be assumed that willingness to participate in a voluntary activity, even when backed by written permission from parents, means that there is acceptance of the possibility of an injury and, therefore, parents will not or cannot take action in the event of one occurring. Such permission is of value but may not necessarily be a defence in law.

Nor should it be assumed that children will be fully aware of the nature of the activities undertaken and the extent of all the risks involved, or that parents are in a position to understand the risk levels inherent in the activities and the way they are taught.

Defence against negligence

> It is not expected of anyone that s/he should be perfect; only that they should act in a manner which is reasonable in the light of commonly accepted and approved good practice in the context of the activity with which they are concerned.
>
> (BAALPE 1999)

The best defence against negligence is that the teacher can show that what took place in the lesson conformed to what might be termed standard or good or 'Regular and Approved' practice.

¤ *Checklist for 'Regular and Approved' practice*

1   The form and content of the lesson should reflect what is seen to be standard practice for pupils of the same age in schools throughout the whole country.
     This is particularly important in subject aspects such as educational gymnastics that are not normally understood by members of the public or those involved in the law.

2   The lesson content should be geared to the range of ability and experience levels of the pupils in the class and reflect the requirements as laid down in the school's PE policy document and schemes of work devised for each year.

3   Records should be kept of the material covered in lessons and of the assessed progress and current ability levels of all class members. Pupil profiles with reference to particular needs (e.g. medical, disabilities) and the limits of each child's capability (such as strength, mobility etc. as well as skill) should be available.

4   The levels of supervision must be satisfactory.

5   Those responsible for the actual teaching of a lesson must be properly qualified in the subject aspect being taught (e.g. gymnastics) (see *Qualifications and competence* below).

6   Helpers, such as class assistants and volunteer parents, must be fully briefed as to their roles and have the necessary knowledge of safety, accident procedures and risk. The role of helpers should be restricted to encouraging and checking. On no account should they be allowed to adopt an active teaching role e.g. setting tasks, telling children to attempt particular movements, giving full body support.
     Properly trained and qualified instructors or coaches who have been engaged by the LEA or school may be responsible for the lesson content. The roles of the instructor and teacher should be agreed and each must be fully aware of their respective responsibilities. The teacher will always have overall responsibility for the children and the conduct of the lesson (see Adults other than teachers below).

7   Teachers must not leave areas where activities are taking place *under their control* – unless another *qualified* teacher is present. In case of emergencies, pupils should stop work immediately and sit down or stand where they can be seen and away from all apparatus and equipment. Responsible pupils or class assistants or volunteers may be sent for assistance (e.g. in the case of accidents). Litigation actions have been successfully brought on the basis of teachers being absent from the place where an accident occurred.

8   All equipment must be in good condition and, where appropriate, properly positioned and secured.

9   Operating conditions must be satisfactory and free from perceived danger (e.g. a slippery or uneven surface).

10 Pupils and staff should be suitably attired and prepared for the subject aspect (see Chapter 2).

11 In the absence of medical evidence to the contrary, pupils suffering from injuries and skin conditions or who show signs of illness must not take part.

12 The school health and safety policy document must include PE and show that risk assessments have been made and should be regularly updated. The document should show who is responsible for risk assessment in PE and what checks are to be made, when and by whom.

13 It is vital that the school has, and parents are informed of, a policy on physical contact with pupils (e.g. on supporting in gymnastics).

14 All teachers should be fully aware of the content of the school PE policy documents and be absolutely clear as to their own responsibilities, both specific to a particular lesson and of a more general nature.
15 Lessons should be planned and, along with schemes of work, should make clear references to safety precautions, minimising risk etc. This is particularly so when new activities or procedures are introduced.
16 Any changes in regard to risk management and practice should be communicated to teachers immediately they are made and checks carried out to ensure the message has been received.

Staff should have the opportunity to undertake in-service training in risk management and to discuss practice and procedures in staff meetings. It can be helpful to discuss cases of negligence and keep abreast of the latest information on good practice, possibly involving expert witnesses or LEA advisers in courses and discussions.

TEACHING

The value of good practice in providing a very firm foundation for safety and in avoiding accidents cannot be underestimated.

Creating a calm and ordered *routine* prior to, during and after each activity session is most important. For example:

- In gymnastics, it is important to organise groups so that they sit in straight rows in designated positions adjacent to, but *not* in contact with, each set of apparatus when listening to comment or taking part in discussion.
- Pupils must be taught to move in an orderly fashion. Allowing pupils to charge from point A to point B promotes a careless approach to PE and increases the chance of accidents occurring.

All children should know precisely what to do in a given situation. Instructions must be repeated, if necessary a number of times, until checks show they are fully understood.

Pupils should be taught about the *risks* involved in taking part in activities and in regard to using apparatus and equipment and, specifically, not to act foolishly.

- Checks should be carried out to ensure that the pupils have understood what they have been told of the possible dangers, at a level that can be expected from a particular age and intelligence range. Information on risk should be given at different points in the lesson and repeated as necessary.
- Pupils must be made aware of all safety procedures and risks in relation to clothing and footwear, the wearing of jewellery etc. and appreciate the reasons for imposing rules.
- A culture of consideration for others, in respect of safety, should be created.

In summary, consideration should always be given to both *Teaching Safely* and *Teaching Safety*.

Pupils must, by following the correct developmental steps, be properly prepared for whatever activities are being undertaken.

Good teaching practice cannot prevent all accidents from occurring. It can, however, go a very long way in ensuring that a very large percentage of those accidents that are avoidable are actually prevented. It is the first and most important plank in the whole safety edifice.

NB GOOD PRACTICE IS SAFE PRACTICE.

Legislation affecting physical education

The Health and Safety At Work (HSW) etc. Act 1974

Schools, although not specifically mentioned, come under the aegis of this act.

Employers (the LEA for most schools; the governors in Voluntary Aided or Foundation schools, proprietors, trusts etc. in independent schools) are bound in law to provide a safe environment for all *employees*, including teachers, paid class assistants and anyone contracted to work in the school in a coaching capacity. The employers must produce and revise, when appropriate, a policy document covering health and safety. This document should show how the arrangements will be carried out and brought to the attention of teachers, assistants and coaches. A safe environment must be provided and this applies to lessons in physical education and, by extension, will affect pupils. For example, the floor in the hall and playground surfaces must be maintained in good condition if the staff and children are to be able to operate safely on them.

The Management of Health and Safety at Work Regulations (MHSWR) Act 1992 (revised 1999)

This act is, in effect, an extension of the HSW Act of 1974. It requires employers to constantly monitor and review the arrangements made for health and safety throughout the school premises. The same applies to other premises where school PE activities take place such as swimming baths, sports centres and outdoor adventure areas.

Managing Health and Safety in Schools (HSE) Act 1995

This document summarises the requirements of the above acts and, along with other legislation, is covered in chapter 4 on *Risk management principles*.

Risk assessment and management

Since 1993, when the MHSWR became operative, employers have been required to identify and assess the level of risk that teachers, assistants, coaches and pupils may be subjected to when working on school premises. In practice, in primary schools, an assessment of risks in PE is usually made by the head teacher in consultation with, initially, the subject curriculum leader and, finally, all members of staff.

If risks are found to be too high, changes must be made so that they are reduced to acceptable levels or, if that is not possible, a task or activity must no longer take place.

NB Assessment and management and producing a school policy on risk is covered in depth in chapters 4 and 5.

Qualifications and competence

In law, the only requirement for someone to *be responsible for*, as opposed to *teach*, a class in an aspect of physical education in an LEA school is that they have qualified teacher status (normally, a Teaching Certificate, a BEd, a BA or BSc with an in-built teaching element, or a PGCE).

In practice, it is necessary for those who teach a given activity to be totally *competent* to do so. Teachers should be familiar with the material, progression, approach, evaluation of and, above all, the safety aspects of a PE subject area up to the level at which they are going to teach it.

To become competent to teach all the PE areas now embraced by the National Curriculum (even with swimming taught, as is usual, by ASA or STA qualified teachers), teachers need to have experienced an in-depth professional course as part of ITT or relevant in-service courses.

Unfortunately, few primary teachers who have qualified in recent years have enjoyed ITT courses in PE of the necessary depth and range. This is because the current NC orders only require primary oriented trainees to cover the three 'core' areas plus ICT and one other subject. In addition, prior to that, the number of hours given to Professional PE on many ITT courses had been cut to the bone. In the last few years, it seems that an increasing number of primary NQTs have begun their teaching career with little in-depth knowledge of how to teach PE.

Head teachers should attempt to establish precisely what was covered in any professional PE courses taken by an NQT. It is strongly advised that the head teacher should consult with LEA advisory staff or qualified consultants and then decide exactly what aspects of what PE areas the teacher is competent to teach. Special care should be taken over areas such as gymnastics, games played with implements, hard balls etc. and, if not taken exclusively by a specialist instructor, swimming. For example, teachers who have not covered gymnastic apparatus work in sufficient depth should never be allowed to teach it.

Teachers who have not covered aspects in sufficient depth must not attempt to teach them. If asked, they should point out that they lack the necessary expertise and that it would be wrong to take the risk. Pupils will be endangered and staff may be found liable in the event of accidents.

In the short term, active steps should be taken to ensure that teachers do become competent to teach, at a minimum, the core areas of PE. In regard to the 'danger' areas and if an NQT has done no PE at all in training then help must be sought immediately. Teachers can be helped via induction sessions, on- and off-site in-service courses and through hands-on help provided by advisory teachers or consultants.

Where PE coverage in ITT has been minimal or a limited amount of help has been provided by advisory or school staff, only very simple 'safe' activities using floor, mats and small apparatus may be attempted. Material at this level may be obtained from books, published schemes, videos etc. As knowledge develops, more demanding activities, which without proper handling may be hazardous, may be attempted.

If there are any doubts regarding what is advisable, help should be sought from PE advisory staff or consultants. All staff must learn that

IT IS NEVER WORTH TAKING A CHANCE.

Teachers would normally be expected to take LEA or National Governing Body courses in order to teach, assist in teaching or organise extra-curricular clubs in certain PE aspects, such as swimming or Vaulting and Agility gymnastics.

Continuing professional development to update on methods and equipment is required if the pupils are to operate in a safe environment.

Adults other than teachers (AOTTs)

It is now common for adults other than qualified teachers to assist with physical education in a school. Properly trained and supervised, such AOTTs can contribute a great deal to raising standards and widening experience for pupils at all levels of the ability spectrum.

They may be local authority or national governing body of sport development officers, school sport coordinators or partnership managers, qualified coaches or instructors, parents and other volunteer helpers, teacher assistants, community sports leaders or FE college or sixth form students taking junior leader type awards.

Depending on their qualifications and experience, they may be responsible for delivering lessons or extra-curricular sessions both on and off the school site, assist a class teacher with the core curriculum or help with teams or clubs in the evenings or weekends.

There are a number of important points to consider.

Responsibility

The employer (LEA, governors, trustees) is responsible for any kind of input made by any AOTT (DfES Guidance 0803/2001; see Appendix F). There are three broad categories of AOTTs; contracted staff such as teacher assistants and caretakers or coaches (e.g. swimming instructors working with classes at an on-site or local authority pool), development officers and coaches who are paid by outside bodies, and unpaid volunteers.

Health and safety law makes no distinction between the legal responsibilities of qualified teachers and other contracted school staff (e.g. assistants, caretakers). All permanent staff and any other person who is contracted to the LEA or school are bound by the health and safety policies set out by the LEA and/or governors. Coaches and development officers paid by other bodies and unpaid volunteers only have a general duty of care.

Schools must always ensure that their policies in regard to AOTTs assisting with PE reflect those of the employer.

Screening

Employers, possibly working through the head teacher, should ensure that proper screening is carried out.

Volunteers, coaches etc. must have child protection register clearance. All should be able to prove their fitness to work with pupils through Criminal Records Bureau (CRB) *enhanced disclosure certification*.

It is worth checking to see if any one wishing to work in the school as a coach or volunteer is on an LEA register of approved personnel or, conversely, where such information is available, a register of those who, for a variety of reasons, are not recommended. Great care should be exercised over those who are not on an LEA list or are not known to the school.

Competence and qualifications

Head teachers and governors must be totally satisfied that any person who is to work with children in PE is 'qualified', by training and experience, to discharge the level of 'duty of care' required by the nature of their teaching or assisting.

Any coach, instructor or sports development officer should have a recognised teaching qualification or a coaching award or certification from an appropriate professional body (e.g. NGBs such as British Gymnastics, UK Athletics and the Amateur Swimming Association) or nationally recognised vocational awards.

- The contents of such an award should be checked and deemed to be acceptable by the school and/or the LEA.
- The award or training record should embrace the use of appropriate material and, specifically, a section on how to teach children of primary school age (how to work with a *whole* class, achieve progression across the whole ability range, for example). If the award does not cover work at KS levels 1 and 2, the coach should have attended an appropriate induction or other course relevant to the age group or had suitable tutored experience in the field. If a coach has not attended appropriate courses or had the relevant experience, he or she cannot be said to be competent to teach *safely* and *appropriately* at KS levels 1 and 2. It is therefore recommended that such coaches should not be employed to work with classes until they have attended relevant courses and/or received appropriate 'hands-on' help.

Additionally, coaches who work with selected groups at KS2 should have a qualification that includes tuition on how to work with the type of child selected for the coaching or appropriate assessed experience.

Volunteers must have an appropriate *qualification* or *knowledge of relevant practices* and the *supervised experience* necessary to work at a given level. On no account should a parent be allowed, for example, to coach a team simply because he or she is keen and has a history of playing or watching a sport. It would be necessary to show that he or she has the necessary teaching skills and knowledge of practices, rather than simply experience of playing. In the event of litigation, following an accident, enthusiasm would not be accepted in a court of law as a valid reason for being allowed to take a team.

Appropriate guidance and instruction may be arranged through LEA advisory staff or by taking courses organised by recognised bodies. For example:

- BAALPE, PEAUK, Sports Coach UK and Sport England have developed a two-phase introductory support system for AOTTs. They provide modules at two levels: Stage 1 – an in-school support pack for volunteers without qualifications; Stage 2 – for coaches who already have qualifications (e.g. NGB awards) and volunteers who have completed Stage 1 and gained sufficient experience to progress further. Details from Sport England (see Appendix F).
- Sports Coach UK organise a course on coaching children.

After appropriate induction and instruction, volunteers, such as parents, may assist

- with infant PE lessons in a similar way to teacher assistants. They will work under the *direct supervision* of the teacher on suitable activities (e.g. simple beanbag skills);
- a teacher or qualified coach with team practices etc.

Such volunteers must never 'join in' i.e. play in the games or attempt to support or catch pupils.

Partnerships

If it is proposed to employ someone other than members of staff to teach lesson or extra-curricular activities, either on or off site, at a sports centre for example, it is advisable that a partnership is set up with any agency involved (e.g. a NGB such as British Gymnastics, Youth Sport Trust's 'Tops' initiative or a local authority).

Following discussions with the head teacher and the curriculum leader and, possibly, if appropriate, a class teacher, a detailed breakdown of what is to be done, and in what way, should be agreed between the school and the agency representative and set out in a signed document. A similar agreement should be drawn up with a volunteer coach acting on his own initiative.

More detail on drawing up such an agreement can be found in the document Hampshire County Council Education (1997) *Safety in Physical Education* (see Appendix F).

It is advisable that LEA PE advisory staff or, in the case of non-LEA schools, an appropriately qualified consultant should be consulted when setting up a scheme or checking the competence of AOTTs.

School policy on safety and risk

All AOTTs must be made fully aware of and agree to put into practice the school's policies on safety and risk (including assessment procedures) (see *Supervision* below)

Child protection procedures

AOTTs should be made aware of, and work within, the child protection procedures that have been set up by the LEA or the school. Of particular importance is the policy on physical contact with a pupil (see chapter 5, *Physical contact and providing support for pupils*).

AOTTs should ensure that there is no possibility of false accusations being made in regard to inappropriate contact and verbal suggestions. As is the case with teachers, coaches and volunteers should never work with a single pupil and, in circumstances when not being directly observed by a member of staff, should consider very carefully whether to operate with twos and threes.

Setting up a programme

Before starting work, all AOTTs should be given information on school procedures, policies regarding behaviour and punishment and dealing with accidents, as well as risk, safety and child protection as outlined above.

Details of the work to be covered and how it should be developed should be discussed and agreed by the AOTT and the school PE curriculum leader or class teacher.

Supervision

AOTTs must never operate without supervision. As stated, AOTTs do have a duty of care but, whatever their levels of expertise and the circumstances, a qualified teacher should retain overall responsibility for the pupils at all times and, therefore, should always be present in a capacity that allows him or her to intervene if necessary.

A suitably qualified and experienced coach, contracted to the LEA or school, may assume responsibility for lesson content and direction of the pupils. Initially, the teacher should either work alongside the coach or remain in close contact with the class. When it is clear that the coach has the necessary competence to work effectively and *safely* with the pupils in that particular class or group, the teacher may operate at greater distances away. As is the case with a teacher taking PE lessons, a higher duty of care will be expected from a coach operating in this way.

As volunteers are not legally bound by the health and safety requirements laid down by the employer, they should always work alongside a qualified teacher. This applies even if the volunteer is very well qualified (e.g. a retired teacher with a PE background) and able to make a major contribution.

A person under the age of 18 is a minor and as such cannot be responsible for groups of children, however small. A minor can only work under the *direct* control of a teacher and in such a way that he or she can be continuously observed and guided.

Key responsibilities of the coach or volunteer

The coach or volunteer should

- use only facilities and equipment as agreed;
- treat in total confidence necessary information given on pupils' health and behavioural problems;
- be fully cognisant with the emergency procedures to be followed in the event of an accident;
- in regard to first aid, have access to equipment and know exactly where it is kept and, specifically in respect of a coach assuming some responsibility for an extra-curricular activity, in the absence of a member of staff with a first aid award, possess an up-to-date qualification.

Monitoring AOTTs

Checks should be made to ensure that what has been agreed in regard to content and teaching mode is actually being carried out. If it is apparent that paid coaches or volunteers do not have the necessary expertise or are not conducting lessons in the way that was agreed when a contract was signed or a partnership set up or are ignoring the school's policy on safety and risk in PE or compromising pupil safety in any way, they should not be allowed to keep working with children. They may be asked to undertake further training or be permanently excluded, depending on the circumstances.

Outside centres

In the case of an outside centre, procedures and the teaching or coaching environment should be carefully assessed for safety. If any of the above requirements are not met, either the necessary changes must be made or the partnership abandoned.

Informing parents

Parents should be informed of the nature of the involvement of AOTTs.

Insurance cover

There should be full insurance cover for all AOTTs. Employers or head teachers should check to ensure that insurance to cover liability is provided by the LEA, a government agency, a national governing body, the school or other bona fide organisation.

Such insurance should embrace all who are active in any way in helping the school in its curricular and extra-curricular programme. For example, this should include parents who use their cars to transport pupils to other sites (e.g. school sports team members). Parents of the pupils who are being transported should be informed and written consent obtained.

Further guidance

At the time of going to press, BAALPE and the DfES are working on a set of comprehensive guidelines on the employment of AOTTs in school physical education programmes. It is intended that these guidelines be made available to all schools.

Trainee teachers

Trainee teachers on school experience *must* always be supervised by a qualified teacher. It is no longer acceptable to allow trainees to take PE lessons on their own on the basis of potentially hazardous apparatus and equipment not being used.

It is recommended that the school or class teacher establish exactly what has been covered in PE, to date, on the ITT course being taken by the trainee. The trainee should only be asked to teach what has been covered in ITT or, if based on material obtained from books, videos or other people, including members of the school staff, is accepted as being safe by the class or head teacher e.g. simple gymnastics floor work or basic beanbag activities.

Trainees must be informed of the school policies on health and safety with special reference to practice and risk in PE and actions to be taken in the event of accidents occurring or emergencies arising.

Curriculum leaders or class teachers should check lesson plans to ensure that proper regard has been paid to safety and matching the material to the pupils' abilities.

2　The teacher and the child

This chapter is concerned with factors that are common to the organisation and teaching of all the NC practical areas. Although there are overlapping elements, for simplicity the chapter has been split into two sections:

A　The *child's* fitness to undertake a given activity
B　The responsibilities of *teachers*.

Section A: The child

Ability levels

Lesson material should be deliberately matched to each pupil's current skill level and potential. This is called *differentiation* and may be done by setting tasks that

- allow for a range of different responses, partly in respect of degrees of difficulty (e.g. in gymnastics), *or*
- cater for different levels of ability by varying conditions on what is basically the same task (e.g. in games), *or*
- are different for selected groups or individuals.

Matching capability to task difficulty in this way is vitally important, ensuring that there is a high probability of safe execution, i.e. higher than when all pupils are treated as if they had the same ability.

Danger and risk

Pupils must always know exactly what they have to do, under what conditions, and be aware of the limits of the operating area.

Pupils should be instructed about the possible dangers in all aspects of physical education that are covered in a school and, specifically, those that apply to particular activities or lessons.

Instructions should be repeated and pupils' understanding continually checked. A 'culture' of risk avoidance and sensible behaviour should be developed.

Dress

Pupils must always wear clothing and footwear that is suitable for the activity and the conditions under which the activity is taking place.

Indoors

Normally gymnastics and dance and, at KS1, small apparatus and games:

- T-shirt, vest or sports shirt; pants or shorts; leotard.
- Bare feet (if the floors are clean and in good condition), gymnastic slippers or clean trainers with flexible soles and a good grip.

Outdoors

Games, athletics, small apparatus, adventure etc.:

- T- or sports shirt; pants or shorts/games skirt and/or tracksuit.
- Pupils should be allowed to wear additional clothing in cold weather in order to keep warm. Sweatshirts, jumpers, tracksuits and leggings are acceptable. If children are cold, attention suffers and accidents are more likely to happen.
- Trainers or boots according to activity and conditions.

   NB Specialist protective clothing may be required under certain conditions in certain games. This topic is covered further in chapter 8.

Hair

Loose, long hair should be securely tied back using appropriate cloth, elastic bands or ribbons, separately or in combination.

Proscribed clothing

On no account should

- normal shoes or boots, sandals or any footwear with slippery plastic soles be worn.
- indoor work be done in stockinged feet
- Any activity be attempted
   o   in dresses, long or normal length skirts or loose tops (these can catch, impede or fall over the head) or long trousers or jeans (these are restrictive and will impede movement)
   o   with a blouson, tracksuit top etc. hanging open (they can catch on apparatus or hit other pupils)
   o   in trainers with loose soles; boots with studs that are irregular or sharp; with tongues that are loose; laces too short or too long and not properly done up.

   It is important to ensure that laces stay tied, Velcro straps are in position, and hair is tied up *throughout* the lesson.

Cultural differences

Some religious beliefs require the wearing of certain forms of clothing. Satisfactory arrangements should be made either with parents or with group leaders to ensure that, in conforming to these requirements, the pupils can still operate safely.

Personal effects including jewellery

The wearing of items such as medallions, necklaces, badges, earrings, studs, pins, bracelets, rings, watches, in fact everything other than prescribed clothing, is very dangerous. Every effort should be made to ensure that such items are removed in all PE lessons and extra-curricular activities.

It is worth noting that jewellery has been the cause of a number of serious accidents, including ear lobes being torn off.

If there are occasions when it is not possible to remove jewellery such as earrings, it may be possible to participate if the items are covered with surgical tape (not Elastoplast). The mode of the participation would depend on the activity. For example, it would not be advisable to do gymnastics on large apparatus with body piercing studs in the ears or stomach in place, even if taped, and alternative tasks may have to be created.

If it is not possible to take an active part, the child should sit out and be involved through question and answer. Hopefully, this situation would only be temporary.

Protection from the sun

Over exposure to sunlight, particularly in mid-summer, can be dangerous. Particular care should be taken regarding the time spent out in the open.

- Sports days are best held in the evening or early morning.
- Lessons in strong sunshine should be kept short.
- Particular regard should be shown to light-skinned pupils.
- If long periods may be spent in strong sun, as, for example, in a cricket match, long sleeved shirts and hats with wide brims should be worn.
- Blocking cream, provided or approved by the parent of the child, may be applied if it is known that exposure may be particularly harmful or lengthy.

Spectacles

There can be danger in wearing glasses. Elastics can be used to secure them in place, making activities like gymnastics and athletics safer. Glasses with unbreakable lenses should be worn and are absolutely essential when playing ball games with anything other than a soft ball.

Informing parents

Schools should ensure that all parents are fully aware of the policies on kit and jewellery, the reasons for adopting them (in regard to minimising danger), and the action that will be taken if any child or parent is not prepared to conform to the rules laid down. Ideally, parents should be informed of the policies before their children first come to the school and reminded at intervals via reports.

Health

It is crucially important that pupils are 'fit' to take part in either the whole or designated parts of the PE lesson.

Permanent and temporary disabilities

Teachers must be fully aware of any disability or ongoing condition (e.g. heart, diabetes, asthma) that may affect

*   whether a pupil may take part in a given activity
*   the limits of what the pupil may be expected to do – in regard to, for example, task nature and difficulty, or length of time that may be spent working.

Lists of pupils with ongoing medical problems should be issued to class teachers who, in turn, should ensure that all others who take the class for PE (e.g. swimming instructors, teacher trainees on school experience) are informed. Such lists must be constantly updated in regard to newly developed conditions and new pupils.

Teachers should know what action to take in the event of a pupil suffering an attack of, for example, asthma or epilepsy. Particular care should be taken over pupils who return after a long illness. Initially, activities may have to be modified or less time spent on them.

Excusing pupils

The school should have a policy with clear criteria for excusing pupils from doing PE.

All parents should be made fully aware of this policy.

Notes from doctors, nurses and other medically qualified personnel would normally be accepted as valid reasons for excusing pupils. Where it is not clear if the note is underpinning a request to be excused *all* or *some* activities, wholly or partially, until further notice, clarification should be asked for.

Notes from parents should be seen as *requests* to be excused and treated on merit. It is possible to excuse a pupil completely or for certain activities depending on the nature of the request. Where there is some doubt, it is recommended that, in the present litigious climate, teachers should definitely err on the side of caution.

Parents may be asked for more information, including reports from medical personnel, and advice may be sought from the LEA's medical officers. At times, it may be necessary to contact PE advisory staff for help in interpreting the limitations imposed by a given condition i.e. if activities can be attempted at all and, if so, with what modifications and for how long.

Teachers should be prepared to stop pupils from taking part in all or some lesson activities, even when a request to be excused has not been made by parents. If, for example, there is evidence of clear discomfort, bandaging, serious bruising or grazing or temporary disorders such as feeling sick, teachers should not allow pupils to participate. Many pupils are so keen to take part that they will claim to be fit to do so regardless of their actual condition.

Colds

Colds, often the most common reason cited by parents when requesting non-participation, are a special case.

Some schools have argued that, if a pupil is in a fit state to attend school, he or she should be able to do PE. Such schools have insisted that pupils with colds take PE, sometimes having first obtained the backing of the school medical service.

Another policy that has been tried is that pupils with, or claiming to have, colds are told that they must take part but that they should only do what they feel capable of. The system has proved very successful with the majority doing all or most of the activities. As the proviso allowing the pupil the decision on actual participation will be acceptable to the majority of parents, it is recommended that such a policy be seriously considered.

Pupils with special educational needs

> When teaching physical education to pupils with special educational needs, a special kind of teaching expertise and the right degree of care is required.
>
> (BAALPE 1996)

There is a statutory requirement to ensure that all pupils with special needs are given opportunities to participate in PE in ways that allow them to realise their abilities to the full.

There may be particular problems in regard to pupils with disabilities where teachers should provide

> ... adapted, modified or alternative activities or approaches to learning in physical education and ensuring that these have integrity and equivalence to the National Curriculum and enable pupils to make appropriate progress.
>
> (DfES and QCA 1999)

Schools, using the SEN Code of Practice, must establish needs in regard to PE and how they can best be met, with complete safety. This may range from simplification of instruction, greater differentiation and more checking and surveillance to the need to learn specific techniques on how to assist children suffering from certain disabilities and what sort of activities they can attempt, in what way and to what degree. Importantly, teachers need to know how to respond in an emergency situation. Some is commonsense and much can be gleaned from special needs co-ordinators, medical and other advisers and parents. In some cases, it may be necessary to employ a specially trained assistant or for the teacher or class assistant to attend a course.

It will not be possible, within the scope of this book, to cover all the needs of pupils with disabilities and adaptation of activities, but the following general points are very important.

Consultation

Before a pupil begins a PE programme, in order to establish a medical profile, there must be consultation between the teacher, parents, any professionals involved including doctors and, possibly, the pupil. The limits of what is possible must be established and, particularly, any activities identified that may be injurious to the performer.

Teacher confidence

Teachers must be confident of what they are planning to do with special needs pupils.

School policy

The school's Health and Safety policy documents must make specific reference to special educational needs pupils and their participation in PE.

Special first aid procedures

The school's accident and first aid procedures may have to be adapted, particularly in regard to provision of emergency treatment.

Where pertinent, specific information on special needs is given in the subject area chapters that follow.

It is strongly recommended that all schools purchase a copy of the BAALPE publication *Physical Education For Pupils With Special Educational Needs in Mainstream Education* (see Appendix F). It contains a wealth of information on safety in regard to all PE curriculum areas and all forms of disability and needs, plus a guide to books, videos and other sources on teaching and activities.

Section B: The teacher

Teachers must be fully aware of all their responsibilities. (NB Much that concerns teachers is included in chapter 1 under negligence and qualifications.)

Routines

Establishing good procedures which are always adhered to can help a great deal in creating a safe environment.

The tone of a lesson is established prior to activities *beginning*. Key elements include:

- Calm, orderly changing procedures.
- A well-controlled and quiet mode of moving from classroom to hall, field or playground with the teacher keeping the whole class under observation throughout.
- Making clear what is expected on arrival at the activity area.
- Having equipment ready.

These elements help to create the conditions that are conducive to safe practice.

Teachers should ensure that pupils always work within the parameters that have been set. Work should be stopped and the class reminded, or individuals or groups reprimanded separately, if they exceed their remit. If it is necessary to repeatedly stop an activity in order to guarantee safety, this should be done. Occasionally it may be deemed necessary to change operating conditions or an activity altogether.

It is tempting to turn a blind eye to small transgressions but, if left unchecked, they multiply in number and scale and, ultimately, may lead to problems in regard to both the quality of the work and compromising safety.

Teachers must always gain the attention of the *whole* class and ensure that all have listened to and understood what is required of them.

Bullying

Bullying (e.g. kicking and pushing in football, dislodging or blocking pupils in gymnastics) and the emotional effects it engenders, often reflected in a lack of concentration, can be very dangerous. Good practice, full control and keen observation should ensure that it does not take place.

Lesson content and teacher knowledge

Teachers must only include activities that they are competent to teach safely and that are within the capacity of those pupils who will be attempting them. This is vitally important (see chapter 1, *Qualifications and Competence*).

Properly planned, interesting, varied and well-paced *lesson content*, matched to individual needs and that maintains motivation, is the first requisite to safe practice. Boredom can lead to mischief, often a precursor to accidents.

Teachers should have regular opportunities to update their knowledge of teaching techniques, material and, specifically, safe practice in the handling and setting up of apparatus.

Operating conditions

Before commencing a lesson, teachers must check that

- pupils are in a 'fit' state to take part (see Dress and Health in the previous section);
- surfaces and operating conditions are acceptable (chapters 3, and 6 to 12);
- anything that is attached to a wall or has sharp angles and is deemed to be a possible hazard is padded or cordoned off;
- all equipment not in use is safely positioned (chapters 3, and 6 to 12);
- apparatus is in good condition, in the correct place and, where appropriate, properly secured, *before* the pupils use it.

Start and stop signals

Routines should be established for each type of lesson with all pupils totally familiar with the systems and signals that indicate when they may start working and when they must stop. This is essential in eliminating potential danger. Whistles may be needed outside when pupils are spread over a wide area, in swimming pools and, possibly, in sports halls but not in the hall or gymnasium where the aim is to work quietly.

Risk

Each teacher must be fully aware of the school policy on safety and risk and his or her personal responsibilities in relation to it. This will embrace procedures to be carried out in each lesson, according to where it takes place, the activity, what apparatus is used and the pupils taking part and, possibly, wider responsibilities in regard to making listed checks (e.g. on equipment) on a routine basis (see chapters 4 and 5).

All teachers should be involved in refresher courses on risk in general and PE in particular at least every three years.

Accidents

Hopefully, by following the advice given in this and the following chapters, the possibility of accidents in PE lessons and extra-curricular activities will be markedly reduced. However, not all circumstances leading to an accident can be foreseen and it is almost inevitable that some will occur.

Procedures must be developed for dealing as quickly as possible with accidents that occur in PE.

On-site treatment

Where applicable, an injury or condition should be treated at the school, either at the point the accident occurred or in a room that has been designated for this purpose.

Injuries requiring hospital treatment

Vitally, an emergency procedure must be established for ensuring that in the event of a serious injury requiring hospital treatment transportation is available. This may involve staff cars or the ambulance service.

Pupils experiencing accidents that lead to suspected breakages or severe bleeding, or involve conditions such as shock and loss of consciousness must, when it is safe to move them, be taken to a doctor or hospital.

Procedures should be in place for contacting parents.

All the above procedures also apply if an accident occurs off-site (e.g. at a swimming pool or sports centre).

Accidents on the playground or playing field

The accident may occur on the playground or adjacent field and it must be possible for aid to be brought to the point at which the accident occurred. Some means of keeping a child warm should be available at all times, e.g. a thermal blanket or sleeping bag.

If help is required, an assistant or pupils who can be trusted should be sent while the teacher looks after the class.

Staff qualified in first aid

The names of staff who are qualified in first aid should be known to all teachers (including supply teachers) and ancillaries, and should be displayed at a point where they can be seen by all (e.g. reception area or hall).

Accident reports

If the accident is serious, leading to death or hospital treatment or absence from school for three days or more, a report must be made by the LEA or school to the HSE by telephone and, within seven days, in writing, using form (HSE) F2508.

The following information is required in an accident report:

- The location and time of the accident.
- The name and status of the injured child or adult.
- Details of the nature of the accident.
- Details of the activity, apparatus being used and the site of the accident.
- Details of the circumstances of the accident.
- Names of those involved and of witnesses.
- Measures taken to promote safe practice and reduce or eliminate risk.
- The experience of the injured party in regard to the activity.
- Any fault in the apparatus or equipment and any environmental factors that may have contributed to the accident.

All accidents in PE should be recorded, regardless of whether an injury of any type was sustained. Information on the circumstances and possible causes can be a valuable aid in regard to making immediate changes or when risk assessments are carried out.

If an accident is serious, the following should be recorded as soon as possible:

- A description of the task and the operating conditions.
- A plan showing any apparatus or equipment involved and its positioning relative to other apparatus, and the exact location of the accident and the positioning of other pupils (if possible specific to the point where the accident occurred, if not then within the general operating area).
- The pupil's ability in regard to the task and, if relevant, the particular movement attempted.
- The teacher's account of what actually happened, if observed. If the accident was not witnessed by the teacher then an account should be provided of the situation when the teacher's attention was drawn to the accident. The accounts and perceptions of any other adult present, other children and the child experiencing the accident should also be recorded.
- It is advisable to take signed witness statements from adults and children mature enough to understand a situation. It may be an onerous task but could prove to be of great value if parents take up the matter with the school or authority or proceed with litigation.
- Details of times, procedures followed, what resulted from going to hospital, and contact with parents should also be recorded.

First aid

All schools must be properly equipped with fully stocked, properly marked first aid boxes. Boxes should be available both for use on the premises and for taking to other sites where curricular and extra-curricular activities are to take place and no first aid equipment is provided.

First aid equipment should always be kept in the same place and be easily accessible from any site on or adjacent to the premises where physical education is taking place (hall, playground, fields). If other sites, such as sports centres, are used, staff should ensure that they know where first aid equipment is kept and that necessary items are in the boxes.

All staff (including ancillaries and supply teachers) and pupils should know where first aid equipment is kept. All staff should have a record of the telephone numbers of doctors and the ambulance service.

One teacher should be responsible for ensuring that first aid boxes are kept fully stocked.

Although there is no requirement in law, it would be sensible if all members of staff within a school have some knowledge of first aid and that a number possess up-to-date qualifications or have recently attended LEA courses (the HSE currently accepts first aid certificates as being valid for three years). This provides additional cover in case of absence or non-availability of trained personnel.

It can also be an advantage to have non-contact staff, such as a secretary, qualified in first aid, as they would not have the problem of dealing with a class at the same time as helping an injured child.

It can be very helpful if a PE specialist, semi-specialist or curriculum leader is fully qualified in first aid, given that a teacher in this position may spend a great deal of time outside the school buildings and site.

Dress

Teachers should dress in a suitable manner for the activity and the nature of their intended role. Changes are necessary both from a safety point of view and to set an example to the children. Teachers cannot expect pupils to conform to dress codes if they totally ignore the requirements themselves.

- Normal shoes or stockinged feet would not be acceptable. Bare feet or trainers indoors, and the latter or sports boots outside are acceptable.
- A shirt or blouse, sweatshirt, pullover or closed track suit top would be suitable depending on the weather but NOT a jacket, top coat or any garment that is loose or open and liable to swing about.
- Skirts, dresses and trousers, as would be worn in the classroom, would normally be satisfactory. If role or conditions demand otherwise, tracksuit bottoms or shorts are acceptable.
- Hair to be tied back if necessary.
- Jewellery to be removed depending on the nature of the role. For example, if supporting in gymnastics, watches, bracelets, brooches and earrings should all be removed.

¤ *Checklist for formulating an accidents procedure*

On-Site treatment

- Are there procedures in place for treating non-serious injuries in school?
- Has a suitable room been designated for treatment of injuries in school?

Injuries requiring hospital treatment

- Is transportation available to take children to hospital?
- Are all staff and children aware of procedures for calling an ambulance?
- Are procedures in place for contacting parents?

First aid equipment

- Does the school have at least two fully stocked first aid boxes?
- Are the boxes easily accessible and in places known to staff and pupils?

Accidents on the playground or playing field

- Can first aid equipment be brought to the point at which the accident occurred?
- Are there means available for keeping a child warm? e.g. sleeping bag, thermal blanket

Staff qualified in first aid

- Are the names of staff qualified in first aid known to all teachers?
- Are the names of staff qualified in first aid prominently displayed?

Accident reports

- Are all staff aware of the need to record and report accidents?
- Are all staff aware of the type of detail that needs to be recorded?
- Do all staff know where to log each accident?

3 The teacher, equipment and environment

All equipment must conform to British Standards (BS) or to the combined European and British standards (BS EN) which are gradually replacing BS.

Checking and maintenance

All gymnastic equipment should be inspected annually by a reputable specialist company. Schools are now responsible for their own maintenance and, sadly, many are cutting corners and only arranging inspections every two or three years or, worse, waiting until equipment can be seen to require repairs. This is a dangerous practice. It is recommended that schools arrange inspections every year.

When equipment is not in full working order (e.g. a splintered bench, a bolt not functioning properly on a climbing frame or bar) it must not be used. The apparatus should be secured so that it cannot be erected, opened or moved and labelled to indicate non-use until repairs are carried out. The temptation to use the equipment in a more limited way, or a section of it, must be resisted.

Other apparatus such as the whole range of small apparatus and games equipment – permanent and portable – must be inspected regularly and repairs carried out whenever necessary (see Appendix D on goalposts).

It is advisable to be extremely careful about who is employed to undertake any maintenance and repairs. All work must be done professionally in order to ensure that equipment is fully up to standard.

All items, including small apparatus, that are split or partially broken must be repaired, if possible, or discarded.

More information on different types of equipment will be found in chapters 6–12.

Storage

Great care should be taken over the placing of equipment when it is not in use.

Primary school halls do not normally have in-built storage areas. Therefore, it is essential that *large items*, such as gymnastic boxes and benches, portable frames, mats and baskets for small apparatus, are not placed where they create obstructions in areas of the hall that are used for other types of activity. This is particularly so where running may be involved (dance-drama, gymnastic floor work and small apparatus).

Where possible, items such as *small apparatus* and games equipment should be stored in specially designated safe areas outside the hall. When such spaces are not available, such apparatus should be placed at one end, or corner, of the hall that has been cordoned off – in such a way that pupils cannot make contact with it by accident.

Benches and other pieces of *gymnastics apparatus* should not be stored one on top of the other. This is highly dangerous. They may be placed, separately, round the sides or ends of the hall, normal way up.

Small items such as balls, bats and hoops should not be left on the floor or behind a bench. *Medium or large balls* should be put in sacks with the openings properly closed. It may be possible to place them in specially created compartments or to fix them to hooks or pegs on the wall. *Hoops* may be placed on static or mobile units, designed for the purpose, or tied in sets with ribbons and, again, attached to the wall. *Small balls*, beanbags, small bats, quoits and skipping ropes may be kept in separate or compartmentalised baskets or boxes (to be carried or wheeled).

Apparatus must be stored in the correct way and in the right place. Mats, for example, should be neatly placed on top of each other, in one or more piles allowing for easy and safe access when next they are to be carried out on to the floor. Throwing them into an untidy heap is dangerous – both when putting them away and on the next occasion when they are required for use.

Transporting and setting-up apparatus

Children should be taught exactly how to carry and set up apparatus.

The moving of apparatus and equipment must be organised so that all pupils know precisely who is taking what, in what way, and to where. Vague orders or suggestions such as *Bring that apparatus here* or *Will some of you go and get* or *We will get the gym apparatus out now – off you go* are not acceptable.

Children should be shown the correct way to lift, lower and move large apparatus, and be given opportunities to practise. The correct methods must always be insisted upon e.g. one KS1 pupil at each corner carrying, not dragging, a mat (see chapter 6, *Apparatus, setting-up – moving apparatus, carrying mats*). NB Pupils should also line up in order to the side of a number of items such as mats so that they never impede the carrying.

Pupils must be strong enough to handle the apparatus they have been asked to carry.

Members of staff should assist where necessary, while still keeping an eye on the remainder of the class.

Pupils must not be allowed to use apparatus or equipment until the teacher has checked that it is in the correct place and, if appropriate, has been set up correctly.

NB Further details on transporting, setting up and checking apparatus are given in chapters 6–12. Chapter 6, on gymnastics, is particularly important.

Apparatus not in use

It is absolutely essential that, during lessons, apparatus that has been taken out but is not currently in use should be placed at least two metres away from the operational area, either on the ground or in designated receptacles, as appropriate.

Apparatus that has been, but is no longer in use, should be removed from the working area. Balls, in particular, but also other small items such as hoops, canes or quoits, if simply left on the floor can lead to accidents (e.g. turning an ankle or slipping). When no longer required, such apparatus must be *carried* and *placed*, as before, on the floor or in the proper receptacle, at least two metres beyond the perimeter of the working area.

Items of small apparatus, small mats or bats should never be simply thrown, rolled or bowled towards the areas where they are to be placed, regardless of how close the

Figure 3.1 KS1 pupils carrying a mat

pupil may be to the storage point or container. Other pupils may be hit and items such as balls and quoits may bounce or roll a long way from or back on to the working area. Items left strewn around present a problem when they are to be used again or returned to permanent storage points.

Children should be schooled in the correct procedure, until it is second nature to return apparatus safely to the correct point in a safe and orderly manner.

Improvisation

Generally, it would be totally wrong to use equipment that has not been designed for a given purpose, particularly if weight is to be supported or contact made with the hands. Such items may not be stable, have protruding screws or nails, or may be splintered.

It may, however, be possible to use low-level stage blocks, either separately or together. Providing they meet the criteria for stability, floor holding, strength and surface condition, such blocks can usefully add to the range of apparatus used in gymnastics and be of use in dance-drama.

Chairs and stools may be used in activities, such as dribbling circuits, where a ball is guided between the legs.

Sharp ended pieces, such as cricket stumps, should never be used as general markers on grass e.g. for running round. Only equipment designed for the purpose, such as skittles, cones and marker domes, should be used.

The use of mats

Mats should

- be of the minimum thickness and type required for a given activity;
- be in good condition, with no splits;
- afford the required grip on the floor.

Details of use specific to activities are given in chapters 6 and 10.

Surfaces

Surfaces should always be

- suitable for the activity;
- in sound condition for physical activities.

All outdoor surfaces

A thorough check of all surface conditions must *always* be made before use.

- Any objects (e.g. glass, bottles, cans, stones, sticks) should be removed.
- Dog faeces can lead to serious illnesses and must always be cleaned up.
- Any holes or cracks should be noted, assessed and, if deemed to be dangerous, either repaired or avoided. If too much of a given area is damaged, no activity should take place.
- Leaves should be removed from asphalt or other artificial surfaces, such as playgrounds, and cricket pitches and squares.

Particular care should be taken over temporary hazardous conditions caused by weather conditions, such as frost.

Playgrounds

Playgrounds should have a smooth, even and non-slip surface. They should be resurfaced either at regular intervals or when assessment shows that they are about to fall short of this standard.

Any *loose grit* or dust should be removed. If there are any serious *cracks* or sections of the surface missing, the affected areas should not be used until repairs are carried out. They must be cordoned off to ensure that they are not used in error. Only the smallest of surface cracks i.e. those too small to allow entry to a toe or shoe edge, are acceptable. Particular attention should be paid to cleaning as dust integrated into the surface undulations can lead to a slippery surface, particularly in wet conditions.

Synthetic surfaces

To avoid skin burns, tracksuit bottoms and long sleeved shirts should be worn for any activity where there is a danger of falling occurring (e.g. invasion games).

Fields

Playing fields should have

- a proper covering of regularly cut grass;
- a reasonably smooth surface and an absence of ridges or hollows that could lead to tripping or loss of balance.

Particular attention should be given to *worn patches*. These should regularly be re-seeded or re-turfed. If such patches do exist and become rock hard or cracked, it would be advisable to avoid playing on them because of the risk of serious grazing and breakages if a toe is caught in a crack.

Indoor surfaces

All floors should be

- very clean;
- smooth and completely free from cracks;
- polished only to the point where a good grip can be obtained when using the correct footwear.

Wooden floors should be free from splinters.

All floors should afford sufficient *spring* for the subject matter being covered. Sprung wooden floors are desirable, especially for dance and gymnastics.

Wet floors are very dangerous indeed. If the whole surface area is wet, the lesson should be postponed until the floor is dry. If a section is wet (due to a leaking roof, for example), it must be cordoned off. It is never sufficient to simply warn children of the danger and ask them to steer clear of the affected area!

Environmental conditions for halls and gymnasia

Halls and gymnasia should be

- properly ventilated and at the right temperature;
- free from excessive glare. Curtains or blinds may have to be partially drawn and positions for addressing the children carefully selected.

Artificial lighting should be properly protected, and *windows* at ground level be either made of unbreakable glass or fully protected. Windows at a higher level should also be unbreakable or protected if games activities are to take place in the hall or any adjacent play area.

4 Risk management principles

Peter Whitlam

What is risk management?

Raising standards in physical education requires teachers to provide tasks of appropriate challenge within acceptable levels of risk. As with all practical areas of experience physical education involves some degree of risk. Managing risk involves both the assessment and, if necessary, further control of any significant risks which may cause harm to pupils or others. This responsibility causes anxiety in a number of teachers, often because of use of the term 'risk'. Risk management is an increasingly used term for what is often called 'safe practice'. These and the term 'good practice' are really interchangeable – good practice is safe practice and safe practice is about managing the risk – or foreseeable possibility – of injury.

Teachers are generally very good at what they do. Every day each teacher makes several decisions, sometimes subconsciously, about the circumstances in which the children in their care operate – in the classroom, the playground or in the physical education lesson. This is managing risk. The vast majority of teachers do it well.

Many teachers also involve the children in the management of risk. This is something all teachers should do. The Reception class teacher who, on entering the hall for a physical education lesson, asks the children to look around and indicate anything that could harm them is exhibiting good practice, teaching safe practice and is educating the children in managing risk. Equally, so is the Year 6 teacher who monitors the class as they devise and manage their own warm-up for the lesson and quietly intervenes to correct and check understanding.

Hundreds of examples of good and safe practice in the management of risk can be cited which all teachers will identify with readily. What do you do if there is glare on part of the water surface in the swimming pool? You move frequently so as to see all parts of the pool bottom at regular intervals. What do you do if the section of the playing field you are going to use has sharp pieces of plastic or metal from drinks containers which have been cut up by the grass mower? You move the class to use a different area. If you teach in a hall with lots of low level glass (even reinforced glass) you organise the activities so that the children 'work into the hall not into the wall' (or windows). If there are sharp projections from furniture, such as the piano or overhead projector stand, you move the item to a position of minimal likelihood of causing injury. The list of common sense examples is endless – and that is what risk management is about – common sense judgements which show reasonable forethought about what could cause injury to a child during the physical education lesson and, if necessary, doing something about it.

As well as these unwritten, pre-emptive actions all teachers make every day, risk management involves an occasional more formal recorded review. This is the statutory aspect of risk assessment. It is the employer's responsibility to ensure that this is carried out. The employer, be it the local education authority (LEA) or the governors/trustees, cannot delegate this responsibility to the teachers but the requirement to carry out the task can be delegated. It is not onerous. It is a task which utilises the everyday judgements described earlier.

Figure 4.1 shows the key factors in maintaining a safe working situation within challenging physical education lessons. Teachers need to think about the people involved, the context of the lesson and the activity involved.

When setting appropriate challenges at an acceptable level of risk to extend individual pupils in their work the teacher has to consider the expertise and experience of the staff and other adults involved as well as the ability, previous experience and confidence of the children. The context of the lesson includes consideration of the facility – such as the examples set out previously, the established routines and procedures for changing, supervision, working or handling apparatus, the size, quality and quantity of equipment and the standards of behaviour and discipline. In presenting the activity the teacher has to consider the class organisation, learning strategy, preparation for the activity and the progression within the lesson as well as from lesson to lesson. When injury occurs and fault exists it is most commonly due to faulty supervision, unsafe environmental conditions or inappropriate activities (Dougherty 1995).

Why is risk management important?

Managing risk in physical education is important because all children are entitled to be taught in a safe and healthy environment. Involvement in the process also empowers

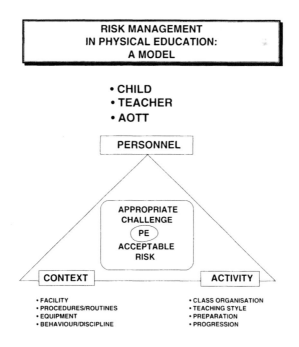

Figure 4.1 Risk management in physical education: a model
Source: Eve, Kirkby and Whitlam 1998

pupils in their own safety. Teachers need a sound understanding of the process because they have a legal responsibility to 'take positive steps to ensure the physical safety of the children in their care' (the Hyppolyte case 1995). Managing risk effectively gives teachers peace of mind.

Analysing why incidents or accidents occur is important in order to improve future practice. When an injury or 'near miss' occurs teachers often reflect only at the level of the immediate, visible cause – the symptom. This superficial level of reflection considers whether the injury was caused, for example, by poor pupil behaviour, equipment not being checked properly or equipment not being used properly – usually the pupil is blamed.

Beyond this the teacher should always reflect more deeply on whether the situation was caused by a lack of knowledge by the pupil or the teacher, a lack of skill, inadequate maintenance of the equipment, normal wear and tear or some other basic cause. This should then be shared with the subject leader to check whether management processes are appropriate – that policies and procedures are sufficiently detailed in order to establish adequate standards overall. If the procedures, programme and policy detail are adequate then the individual teacher may be able to prevent future similar occurrences through some form of continuing professional development.

Analysing accident report forms to identify whether common causes exist is good practice. Regularly but briefly considering safety in staff meetings may eventually lead to the very good practice of also sharing 'near misses' – where injury almost occurred. From this the management analysis of whether policies and procedures are sufficiently detailed may then lead to more consistent safe practice.

How is a formal, recorded risk assessment most effectively done?

Formal recorded risk assessments are most effectively done:

- As a whole staff activity rather than by one person – this draws on the whole experience of the staff and may make less experienced or less confident teachers more aware of situations.
- In situ – in or on the facility itself. The staff can then look around and share views as to what may cause injury and, if deemed to be a significant risk, what can be done to reduce the risk to a more acceptable level.
- When based on existing documentation, procedures and practice – good, safe practice will already be set out in the documentation for physical education. Doing a risk assessment is not about re-inventing the wheel by having to write down everything again. The staff should be aware of what are the documented procedures and routines and check whether these are sufficient to maintain a safe working situation or whether FURTHER, ADDITIONAL precautions are necessary.

The level of awareness expected of teachers is in relation to their expertise. Reasonable anticipation and forethought is expected of a generalist primary school teacher. A higher level of awareness is expected of a teacher who is deemed to be a specialist through initial or continuing professional development. Yet higher expectations are set for anyone who specialises in a particular activity which would take children beyond the expected levels of attainment in the national curriculum, such as that in clubs where the child is operating at a level of relative excellence in relation to others of her/his age.

An outline of the legal framework within which teachers work

Talking about 'the law' can cause great concern for some teachers. At the most basic level the law requires teachers to:

- Teach safely – having reasonable anticipation, forethought and observation skills to a level established by case law over the years and by the requirements of the Health and Safety at Work etc. Act, 1974.
- Teach safety – as set out in the Education (Consolidation) Act, 1996 and the National Curriculum 2000 programmes of study for physical education.
- Have the class control to stop a potentially hazardous situation becoming realised – as set out in Section 37 of the Teachers' Pay and Conditions.

Teachers work within a complex legal framework and are dependent on their employer and the senior management in the school to establish a protective system within which the teacher can work for the benefit of all concerned.

The Health and Safety at Work etc. Act 1974, clearly places the responsibility for carrying out health and safety checks – such as ensuring risk assessments are done – on the employer. The employer cannot delegate this responsibility but may require the teacher to contribute to the tasks related to health and safety.

The 1974 Act requires the employer to provide a safe place of work and safe systems of work. This means a safe working environment and the implementation of a safety policy. The employer must also provide training as appropriate to ensure that the policy can be put into practice effectively.

In more detail the Management of Health and Safety at Work Regulations 1999, sets out the requirement for a risk assessment to be carried out and to record that assessment where there are more than five employees. In practice this means that every school must carry out a documented risk assessment as it is the employer's responsibility and the LEA will have more than five employees. In the rare situations where less than five employees may exist in an independent school it is good practice to document risk assessments anyway.

The Management Regulations also define a 'significant injury' which helps define a significant risk. A risk assessment requires significant risks to be addressed. Low-level risks need to be noted and monitored to ensure they do not worsen but existing practice is sufficient where low-level risks exist. A significant injury is one which would require at least three days off work or off school or one which requires a visit to a hospital for any reason for any length of time. So, any hazard that could cause this level of injury is deemed to constitute a significant risk which needs to be addressed immediately to reduce the level of risk and thus the level of any subsequent injury.

Talk of legal issues should not feel threatening as the responsibility lies with the employer who must provide guidance and appropriate professional development. Also, the plethora of principal and subsidiary legislation which impinges on safe practice in physical education is largely common sense. For example, the Health and Safety First Aid Regulations which were revised in 1997 simply define first aid; set the minimum requirements of at least one suitably stocked, identifiable and easily accessed first aid container; require an appointed person to take charge of first aid arrangements who need be qualified only if there is a large number of employees (not pupils) and requires the provision of notices and other information on first aid arrangements for employees. Off-site activities need the availability of at least a travelling first aid kit. It is logical that records of aid given are kept and it is sensible only to give aid to the level of qualification and expertise held. Arrangements beyond these minimal requirements are based on risk assessment. Teachers reflecting on these regulations will realise that this is common sense and will recognise that the systems operating in their schools fulfil the legal requirements without placing any undue responsibility on their shoulders.

The recommended format for a written risk assessment given in this chapter addresses the main areas which the law requires to be included in an assessment. Teachers need not worry about the law and should simply think around the prompts included in the risk assessment guidance in this chapter.

The Health and Safety Executive (Managing Health and Safety in Schools, 1995) summarise the functions of teachers and management very clearly. In essence:

- a class teacher should:
    o follow set policy and guidelines
    o check that work areas and equipment are safe
    o participate in inspections and risk assessments
    o report problems to the subject leader
- the subject leader should:
    o manage day-to-day subject health and safety issues in relation to school and subject policies
    o regularly review procedures
    o carry out regular inspections and risk assessments
    o report to the head teacher on inspections and assessments, passing on relevant safety information
    o check whether action is taken to safeguard pupils, colleagues and other visitors
    o possibly arrange staff professional development
- the head teacher:
    o manages all day-to-day health and safety matters
    o ensures regular inspections and assessments are carried out
    o submits inspection and assessment reports to the employer
    o ensures that action is taken, within the realms of possibility, on day-to-day practice
    o passes on health and safety information to appropriate people
    o identifies staff training needs
    o liaises with governors and professional association safety representatives on policy and problems
    o carries out any relevant investigations.

The process of assessing risk

Risk assessment involves seven stages:

1   Decide what requires a risk assessment – some prefer to do an assessment of each activity. It is a more streamlined process if each facility is assessed and the other essential aspects included within this. This is the model described later in the chapter.
2   Identify the hazards – by:
    a   looking at each work area
    b   thinking logically through what happens in each activity within the facility

c   including statutory issues such as fire safety and first aid – as indicated in the prompts attached to the suggested format later in this chapter.

It is advantageous for all adults involved in teaching physical education to participate in the assessment as they bring to it the issues specific to the age group of the children they teach as well as their expertise and, possibly, their lack of knowledge which can be developed by taking part.

3   Decide who is at risk – is it one of more of:
   a   The pupils – all of them or particular groups such as the very young or those with special educational needs?
   b   The staff?
   c   Other visitors such as parents, helpers or visiting pupils?
4   Evaluate the risks by:
   a   taking account of existing procedures and precautions to minimise risks
   b   making a professional judgement to estimate the probability of injury by considering the likelihood of injury with the probable severity of injury which may be caused
   c   considering the number of people possibly at risk.
5   Record the findings as you do the risk assessment.
6   Devise an action plan to reduce any significant risks by:
   a   considering whether existing procedures are sufficient
   b   devising additional, appropriate procedures and practices as necessary
   c   prioritise the need for additional procedures or practices if necessary.
7   Inform those affected by any change in procedure or practice through:
   a   Notices or posters
   b   Training
   c   Professional development
   d   Telling them.

The law requires risk to be eliminated in industry. Significant risks are identified by establishing a risk rating based on the multiplication of a factor for the likely severity of injury from the hazard with the likelihood of injury occurring (figure 4.2). Those risks with the highest ratings are addressed first as they are deemed to be the most significant risks.

HAZARD SEVERITY	LIKELIHOOD OF OCCURRENCE
1 Negligible – near miss/minor injury e.g. abrasion	1 Improbable – almost zero
2 Slight – injury needing medical attention – e.g. laceration	2 Remote – unlikely to occur
3 Moderate – more serious injury causing absence from school	3 Possible – could occur sometimes
4 Severe – serious injury requiring hospital treatment	4 Probable – may occur several times – not surprising
5 Very severe – permanent injury/fatality	5 Near certainty – expected.

SEVERITY × LIKELIHOOD = RISK RATING

Figure 4.2 Risk rating

This system may be applied in education but a professional judgement which completes the requirement to calculate the level of risk is sufficient.

The teachers' task is to establish appropriate challenge by reducing risk to an acceptable level for the experience, ability and confidence of the pupils. It is thus more practicable for teachers to simply make a professional judgement about the likely risk in a given situation rather than require to work to a given formula to identify risk ratings as required in industry.

With experience and professional development a teacher recognises whether a situation in a physical education lesson is likely to result frequently in significant injury – that which is likely to cause a visit to hospital or have more than three days off school.

Teachers looking at a situation will immediately decide whether the likelihood and level of injury requires further precautionary action to be taken or whether existing procedures and practice sufficiently covers the risk – this is making a professional judgement. Teachers are doing this every day.

The risk assessment record

There is no set format for a risk assessment. Neither is there a requirement to show how the assessment was done. However, the record must indicate:

- any significant hazards;
- who is affected;
- any further action needed.

It helps if the record is also:

- clear;
- quick to complete;
- sufficient to record all that is necessary.

The assessment needs to take account of current legislation so consideration needs to be given to:

- The personnel:
  - Staffing – ratios, expertise, training, emergency training, non-teachers' roles and responsibilities
  - Medical conditions
  - Pupils with special educational needs
  - Pupil ages
- The context:
  - The facility – the condition of the floor, location of windows, projections, access and egress, clarity of the water in a pool and so on
  - Equipment – needs to be regularly checked and maintained according to the requirements of the activity and of an appropriate size for the pupils
  - Fire regulations – clear access and egress, adequate signs, provision of fire equipment such as extinguishers and/or blankets, a register of those present
  - First aid provision – kits, nominated person responsible, training

- ○ Emergency action – established procedures in case of the need to evacuate the premises
- ○ Transport – embarkation, disembarkation, seating, seat belts,
- The activity:
  - ○ Previous experience, progression, rules
  - ○ Procedures
  - ○ Working arrangements

A suggested risk assessment form can be seen in Figures 4.3 and 4.4.

Completing the form

Figure 4.3 shows the two sides of the suggested format for completing the risk assessment. In column one (Aspects to consider) are a number of sub-headings. These represent the key areas to ask questions about. Figure 4.4 shows the same headings with a number of points to consider. This is more a 'starter for ten' than a definitive list as circumstances in each school will vary. Consider these points about the use of your facility and your procedures. If you feel that there are more issues to consider then add them to the list. If you are happy that current policies and procedures sufficiently address these points then no significant risk exists and a tick should be placed in column two signifying that current procedures are satisfactory. Work through each sub-heading in this way. There is no need to write anything in the relevant section on the form unless you are noting additional considerations as major hazards.

As the form is completed the staff may feel that concern exists about a particular issue within a sub-section. If so, write it in the appropriate space on the form and tick the third column (No) as the current situation is deemed to be unsatisfactory and in need of some attention. When, or if, this occurs then identify who is at risk by writing 'S', 'V' and/or 'P' in column four – remember there may be more than one group at risk even though our thoughts often focus on the pupils.

As the situation is deemed to be unsatisfactory then some action is needed to control and reduce the risk. In columns five, six and seven write in what action needs to be taken, by when and by whom. Column seven also serves as a monitoring check that the action has been taken. Figure 4.5 provides some suggestions for controlling a significant risk, indicating what sort of action may be taken to reduce the identified risk. Note that these are drawn together under the three key factors from Figure 4.1 – people, context and activity. Use these as ideas for action in column five. You may need to add other ideas.

When the form is completed then have it signed and dated, note any necessary action and copy it to the head teacher and governors to show that you have carried out the task. Draw to their attention any action necessary which is beyond the immediate control or influence of the staff.

Inform those affected by any change in practice to ensure that they adopt the changed requirements – use notices, tell those concerned, build the new requirements into planning.

Remember:

- Do the assessment as a group rather than as an individual;
- Do it in/on the facility.

RISK ASSESSMENT FOR PHYSICAL EDUCATION

School:.................................

Work Area:.................................

Aspects to consider (List only actual hazards)	Satisfactory		Who is affected? Staff (S) Pupils (P) Visitors (V)	Is further action necessary? – risk control (Comment)		
	Yes	No		What	By when?	Completed?
Special needs/medical considerations/age/group issues:						
Changing procedures:						
Movement to working areas: (including transport)						
Work area:						
Fire regulations:						

First aid arrangements:					
Lesson organisation/activity:					
Equipment:					
Staffing:					
Emergency action:					

Signed: Headteacher.................................

Subject leader.................................

Date of assessment.................................

Review 1.....................(Date and initial)
Review 2.....................(Date and initial)
Review 3.....................(Date and initial)
Review 4.....................(Date and initial)
Review 5.....................(Date and initial)

Figure 4.3 ¤ Risk assessment for physical education

SOME GENERAL CONSIDERATIONS	

• LEA guidance followed:
• Levels of responsibility according to age of pupils.
 	
Special needs/medicalconsiderations/age/group Issues:
• Individual needs addressed
• Knowledge of medical background
• Extra supervision required
• Expertise of extra adult help
• Implications for following aspects below.
 	
Changing procedures:
• Space available
• Procedures understood
• Showering facility
• Slippery wet floor
• Jewellery
• Hair tied back/loose/beaded hair
• Clothing appropriate to the activity.
 	
Movement to working areas
• Procedures for moving to the area
• Hazards on the way
• Orderly
• Adequate supervision and control
• Appropriate behaviour
• Safe carrying of equipment
• Transport
  – safe embarkation/disembarkation
  – seatbelts used
  – driver requirements/responsibilities
  – no distractions
 	
Working areas:
• Hazard free - sharp corners, piano, chairs etc
• Sufficient space
• Safe surface - grit, glass, splinters, slippery, holes, leaves, ice, water etc
• Dog/horse faeces.
 	
Fire regulations:
• Escape routes clear
• Mat storage
• Extinguishers present and maintained
• Training needed
• Effective emergency communication.
	First aid arrangements:
	• Responsible person
	• Training
	• First aid kits
	• Post-accident procedures.
	
	Lesson organisation:
	• Safe exercise principles - no 'bouncy' stretches/no neck or back over-extension/ warm-up and cool-down
	• Suitability of activity for age/experience
	• Progression in activities
	• Recognised and approved practice
	• Use of available space
	• Group organisation.
	
	Equipment:
	• Use of equipment for purpose it was designed
	• Suitability of equipment for activity
	• Maintenance of equipment
	• Accessibility/storage
	• Handling, carrying, sitting
	• Check before pupils use it
	• Sufficient space
	• Routines for collection, retrieval, changing
	• Procedures for use of equipment.
	
	Staffing:
	• Confidence and expertise
	• Necessary qualifications;
	• Non-teacher support/supervision - e.g parents, coaches, NNEB's, ancillary helpers, students, older pupils
	• Ratios.
	
	Emergency Action:
	• Contact with school/emergency services if off-site
	• Contingency plan needed
	• Supervision of main group and injured party
	• Post-accident procedures
	• Evaluation.

Figure 4.4 ¤ A checklist for the risk assessment form: aspects to consider

- Use the prompt sheet (Figure 4.4) as a 'starter for ten' to identify the issues to be addressed when completing the form.
- Work logically through the session and identify the main issues, deciding whether current practice and procedure is sufficient for all to feel that no significant risks exist.
- Where additional requirements, over and above what is already established practice, are needed then use Figure 4.5 to help identify the further action to be taken.
- Inform anyone affected by changed practice what those changes are.

Carrying out a formal, documented risk assessment at the beginning of each year – or more frequently where the circumstances change for some reason – is not a threatening task. Reasonable forethought is the standard to work to. Ask what could be reasonably expected of someone with your training and experience. Think logically through the exercise. Do it together. Do it for the children. Do it for yourself.

Making the activity safe:
- Teach progressive practices thoroughly
- Explain the inherent risks
- Emphasise playing within rules
- Change the way the activity is carried out
- Stopping the activity
- Avoiding the area
- Using a safer alternative.

Making the equipment safe:
- Buy good quality equipment
- Inspect the facility periodically
- Place warning notice or protective devices where risks exist
- Inspect the equipment
- Repair or service the equipment
- Modify the equipment
- Teach how to use the equipment/facility
- Amend how the equipment is used.

Making the people work safely:
- Provide protective equipment/clothing
- Training – staff qualified and experienced
- Devise appropriate procedures
- Discipline and control
- Develop observation skills.

Figure 4.5 Controlling risks

Points to highlight in school inset on risk assessment

Risk management – what is it?

- good practice/safe practice
- day-to-day decisions
- more formal whole review
- definitions
  - assessment
  - control
  - management
- a model.

Risk management – why is it important?

- why incidents occur
- legal duty – Hippolyte 1995
- empower pupils in own safety
- entitlement to be taught in a safe and healthy environment.

Risk management – how do we do it?

- team activity
- in situ – in the facilities
- based on existing documentation, procedures and practice
- look for FURTHER precautions necessary
- reasonable anticipation/observation
- NOT about writing everything down again.

Risk management – the legal framework

- Health and Safety at Work etc. Act 1974
- Management of Health and Safety at Work Regulations 1999
- other secondary legislation
- common sense
- summary of responsibilities.

Risk management – the process

- Decide what requires a risk assessment
- Identify hazards
  - initial audit of safety documentation and procedures
  - area by area/activity by activity/location
  - logical flow through sessions
  - include statutory issues – fire safety etc.
  - keep it simple
  - group activity – all adults involved in teaching physical education
  - involve pupils during lessons
- Decide who is at risk
  - staff
  - pupils – all/some e.g. SEN
  - other visitors
- Evaluate the risks
  - take account of existing procedures and precautions to minimise risks
  - may use a simple grading system – likelihood and severity – identify probability
  - consider number of people possibly at risk
  - use professional judgement
- Record the findings
  - record as you go
- Devise an action plan to reduce the risks
  - are existing control measures adequate?
  - devise appropriate, additional controls
  - prioritise if necessary
- Inform those affected
  - notices, procedures etc.
  - training.

5   Devising a policy for risk management in physical education

Peter Whitlam

Why have a policy?

No teacher works in a vacuum. All are guided in their routines and practice by whole school documentation.

Documentation is most easily accessible when structured in terms of policy – briefly stating why the issue is important – followed by guidelines – setting out how the policy is put into practice through the application of procedures to be followed.

Documentation relating to safety in physical education is usually contained within the general subject policy and guidelines. Whether written as part of the general policy and guidelines for physical education or established as a discrete statement on managing risk the following principles should be addressed. These will be supplemented by any issues and views specific to the school's circumstances.

A policy statement

The purpose of the policy

- To offer physical education within a well managed, safe and educational context;
- To establish common codes of practice for teachers and pupils;
- To provide common administrative procedures;
- To ensure that statutory and local requirements, other national guidelines such as codes of practice and generally accepted good practice are followed.

A rationale for risk management/safe practice

- To enable pupils to participate in physical education lessons which provide appropriate challenge within acceptable levels of risk but with no danger;
- To provide consistency in practice in order to establish a secure working environment;
- To educate pupils about managing risk to enable them to participate independently in physical activity;
- To fulfil the requirements of the national curriculum for physical education.

The context for risk management

- An environment which is safe for the activity;
- Adequately supervised activities;

- Using regular and approved practice;
- Taking pupils through progressive stages of learning and challenge;
- Build up a system of advice and the practice of warning;
- Use equipment only for the purpose it was intended;
- Provide basic care in the event of an accident;
- Based on forethought, sound preparation and risk assessment.

Further opinion may be found in the nationally recognised guidance in *Safe Practice in Physical Education* (British Association of Advisers and Lecturers in Physical Education – BAALPE – 1999 or subsequent edition).

Guidelines for managing risk

Consider each of the following aspects in relation to the specific circumstances for your school. Supplement the general principles offered according to the personnel, environment and activities in your programmes of activity.

Draft your guidelines in an easily accessible form which indicates clearly what is expected of pupils, parents, teachers and voluntary helpers.

Collate this material into a central resource. The subject leader should then provide each colleague teaching physical education with the documentation relevant to them – the scheme of work for their year group, the assessment forms and the required procedures and routines to be followed to ensure safe practice and a safe working environment.

Specific school procedures

Consider:

- premises design – such as supervising classes from the classroom to the hall;
- notes from parents;
- supervision;
- other issues particular to your school.

Clothing, footwear, jewellery and personal protection

Consider:

- what clothing is acceptable for safe and hygienic participation – the removal of loose items which could get caught on equipment and endanger the pupil;
- footwear to be appropriate, fully laced and safe – barefoot work is best for gymnastics and dance where the floor is clean and splinter-free;
- no jewellery or personal effects to be worn for the safety of the individual and others. If items of jewellery cannot be removed the pupil should only participate if the activity tasks can be adjusted for the individual to make his or her participation safe. There may be instances where a pupil cannot be allowed to participate for their own safety. This is an issue where the local education authority (LEA), governors and head teacher need to clearly support class teachers in their actions

as it is the employer who is responsible for health and safety and the governors and head teacher who have designated day-to-day management responsibility;

- the provision of personal protection, such as shin pads, is a parent's/carer's responsibility. The teacher needs to amend an activity if any personal protection is deemed to be essential but all children affected do not have the required protection. This may be done by amending the task, the equipment, the space or the rules.

Safe exercise principles

Consider:

- the need to warm up before any physical activity – increasing heart rate and some stretching activity;
- cool down after activity – often through slow movement or even the walk back to the classroom;
- avoid rapid or jerking movements;
- do not extend the neck or back too far backwards;
- keep joints within their natural range of movement.

First aid

Consider:

- all staff need to know the nominated person responsible for first aid and how to contact this person in the event of an injury;
- the location of the first aid kits;
- the school's post-accident procedures – informing parents, pupils taken to hospital, completion of records;
- first aid requirements when taking pupils off-site;
- the reporting and discussion of all accidents in order to evaluate existing practice.

Health, medical assessments and records

Consider:

- what checks are made;
- where medical records are kept;
- the procedure for informing class teachers and any replacement staff of relevant individual needs;
- knowledge of emergency aid procedures for pupils at medical risk;
- monitoring the work of pupils susceptible to loss of consciousness such as through epilepsy and adjusting tasks where deemed to be necessary;
- staff to report any injury or impairment which could prevent them from providing adequate safety provision for their class.

Giving medication:

Consider:

- have all staff volunteered to give medicines – it is not a professional requirement
- what are the procedures where a member of staff does not wish to be responsible for giving medication;
- how replacement staff are informed and the policy applied to them;
- inform parents of the procedures;
- where pupils self-medicate what is the procedure;
- teacher awareness of any drugs being taken which may affect sensory-perception or motor control;
- knowledge of any pupil allergies and relevant emergency action required;
- professional development for all staff involved;
- storage and access to medication.

Codes of conduct

Consider:

- whether pupil behavioural codes of conduct are deemed to be necessary;
- informing parents of the detail;
- follow-up action where agreed codes are breached;
- exclusion from an activity where inclusion may be a foreseeable risk to the safety of others.

Pupils with special educational needs

Consider:

- teacher to know the nature of the special need and its implications for physical education experiences;
- planning for the inclusion of wheelchair users within a lesson;
- role and expertise of any support staff;
- informing class teachers and replacement staff of any individual needs;
- any prohibited activities for particular special needs;
- alternative activities;
- monitoring levels of fatigue;
- consultation and discussion with parents to determine an activity profile
- knowledge of the implications for the pupil of any special aids or appliances.

Checking facilities and equipment

Consider:

- check that working surface is clear, clean and dry each lesson so as to provide secure footing;
- prohibit pupils running at speed into walls, doors and windows;
- the prevention of unsupervised access and use of facilities or equipment;

- the need for adequate space for the working group and alternative ways of organising an activity when space is limited;
- guidance about what and how gymnastic equipment needs to be checked when in use;
- children not allowed to work on apparatus until told;
- educating pupils what to check on apparatus
- what checks to be made whilst the activity is going on;
- the system for reporting maintenance needs;
- avoiding the use of condemned equipment;
- procedures for collecting and returning apparatus to a base;
- correct lifting, carrying and placing of equipment to be taught and monitored.

The roles and responsibilities of non-teachers (adults other than teachers – AOTTs)

Consider:

- the legal responsibility and duty of care a teacher carries and cannot devolve;
- the basis on which volunteers and paid coaches work – the level of independence they have and the limits of operation by an AOTT;
- informing parents that their children are being taught by a non-teacher;
- arrangements for disclosure certificates being checked (the former 'police check'), and the level of certificate required;
- routines for ensuring that AOTTs are never alone with a child other than their own;
- checking AOTTs' experience, qualifications and, if necessary, their levels of third party insurance.

Physical contact and providing support for pupils

Consider:

- the employer's policy;
- informing parents that contact in physical education is inevitable and the circumstances in which teacher contact with pupils may occur;
- referring teachers to where in the scheme of work physical contact may occur;
- teachers to inform pupils when contact will occur, the basis of this and contact or support not being made in any way which could be misconstrued;
- the conditions under which pupils may support each other or take part of a partner's weight during an activity.

Higher risk activities

Consider:
  Swimming
- informing teachers taking classes swimming of any regulations set out by the LEA or pool management;
- knowledge of the pool's normal operating procedures and emergency action plan
- maintaining any required staff water safety awards;

- communication between the school staff and the pool staff re numbers involved, confidence levels, temporary individual circumstances, checking all pupils leave the poolside;
- changing supervision;
- observation, scanning and head counts during lessons;
- the non-use of goggles other than for special reasons;
- the characteristics of a distressed swimmer.

Off-site activities
- LEA regulations re staffing ratios, expertise, pre-visits etc.;
- DfES guidance for off-site visits;
- informing parents of the details for any off-site activity;
- essential pupil information for off-site visits;
- contact information in the school;
- first aid and illness procedures;
- roles and responsibilities of volunteer helpers.

Non-participants

Consider:

- pupils to be with the lesson and not left in classrooms;
- alternative arrangements for those not participating in swimming – to be supervised in an appropriate area of the poolside or to remain in school;
- awareness of when pupils are able to continue participation in lessons.

Extreme weather conditions

Consider:

- outside activity in strong sunshine – for limited periods only plus the need for shade, liquid and suncream;
- essential clothing for specific off-site activities;
- wearing additional clothing for outside lessons in the winter.

Transport:

Consider:

- applying LEA regulations;
- minibus management;
- driver regulations and responsibilities;
- seatbelts and no 'three pupils to two seats' arrangements;
- number of staff and voluntary helpers to be involved;
- assessing risk re embarkation, disembarkation and particular points on the journey;
- known points of group dismissal if other than the school site;
- regulations relating to staff use of own vehicles for transporting pupils;
- are codes of behaviour necessary;
- keeping parents and carers informed.

Remember

- documentation is necessary to promote consistent practice through the school;
- more detailed guidance is available for each of the aspects listed here in BAALPE's *Safe Practice in Physical Education* 1999 – check it and add to your documentation where necessary;
- check LEA or other employer guidelines and regulations and include in your routines;
- review the risk management policy and guidelines periodically as a whole staff in order to further promote consistent practice;
- analyse accident report forms to evaluate the effectiveness of your procedures;
- keep parents informed of your policy and procedures;
- subject leaders should monitor whether risk management guidelines are being consistently applied.

6 Gymnastics and dance

This chapter is divided into sections as follows:

A   General principles for gymnastics and dance
B   Dance and gymnastic floor work
C   Apparatus
D   Educational gymnastics
E   Vaulting and agility and awards.

Checklists covering what are considered to be *potentially hazardous* items of equipment and activities and *golden rules* for safe practice in gymnastics and dance are included at the end of the chapter.

Section A: General principles for gymnastics and dance

Basic features

Gymnastics in its different forms can offer an excellent variety of challenges to all children, regardless of ability. These may range from choosing movements and balances of increasing ingenuity and difficulty, through working at different heights to mastering specific vaults and floor agilities. Where there are challenges, there will be risks. As we have no wish to anaesthetise the activity and remove the challenge, we must accept that there may be accidents. We should, however, strive to ensure that they are not of the preventable type.

Dance also offers a range of excellent opportunities for expression and meeting challenges. As many of the same safety factors apply to both, it has been specifically linked to gymnastics in the section on floor work. Elements exclusive to dance are covered separately in the last part of that section, in *Dance*.

Important basic features to consider are:

- the tasks that are possible or advisable in regard to *class numbers*, *age* and *space* available;
- the size, weight and height of the *apparatus* to be used. This must be matched to both the strength and range of ability of the class or group using it;
- the nature and state of the *floor* (see chapter 3, *Surfaces*);
- the *perimeter* of the working area. As running and other dynamic ways of moving may be involved, special care must be taken in regard to objects placed round the perimeter or projecting from the walls. It may be necessary to use padding to cover

buttresses and place cones round objects like pianos. Doors should be closed and designed to slide or open outwards away from the working space.

Clothing

As for all activities, clothing and footwear, if used, should be suitable, hair tied back, jewellery removed, and no sweets or gum to be chewed (see chapter 2, *Dress*).

Specialist Knowledge

In order to offer body support and teach vaulting and agility (including British Gymnastics awards) and other forms of competitive gymnastics, teachers must have either a relevant coaching certificate or have attended a specialist course approved by the LEA or school governors.

Mats

Standard one inch (2.5cm) thick gymnastic mats (now officially termed *foundation* or *floor*, but no longer *safety*, mats by BSI) may be used in all forms of gymnastics and, occasionally, in dance.

- They should always be in good condition – never split – and afford excellent grip on the floor.
- It is vitally important that when they are joined together to form a single larger unit, the adjacent edges are trim and there is *never* a gap between them.
- More information on specific use of mats is contained in *Educational gymnastics* and *Vaulting and agility* below.

Landings

Children should be taught how to land properly (absorb weight etc.) as soon as they are capable.

Section B: Dance and gymnastic floor work

Dance, in all its forms, and basic gymnastic floor work are considered two of the safest aspects of PE. There are, however, a number of factors that must be taken into consideration when planning lessons.

The floor

The floor must be in good condition, totally free from damage and non-slippery. It should afford adequate spring if take-offs and landings are to feature regularly in the programme.

Weight bearing

Special consideration should be given to *weight bearing*. Assisting other pupils to gain height, and moving over bodies, may be a part of a modern educational dance or gymnastics exercise and various partner balances may be taught in gymnastics. It should be ensured that the child who is assisting or taking the weight is strong enough to do so and has proper knowledge of the correct position or mode of movement if stability and balance are to be maintained. The teacher should have had adequate training in whatever is being done and, as with other activities, if there are any doubts an activity should not be attempted.

Dance

In dance and its close relation dance-drama, musical instruments, additional clothing and 'props' may be used.

- If an *instrument*, such as a tambour, or other noise making apparatus is being held, it should be ensured that they are in good condition and that the activity is suitable i.e. holding is compatible with the movement and other class members are in no danger of being hit.
- *Clothing* should be such that there is little restriction and no danger of tripping.
- *Props* should be selected carefully e.g. an umbrella with a metal point would be unsuitable, while a cushion would be acceptable.
- Special care should be taken regarding the positioning of CD players, TVs, radios, special lighting stands and any connecting wires.

Section C: Apparatus

In all forms of gymnastics, it is vitally important that all the apparatus used, including the floor, should be in good condition and properly secured. It is essential that checks are undertaken regularly by whoever has been given responsibility for the equipment, and also by whoever is taking the lesson.

Portable apparatus

All pieces must be stable and secure. Therefore:

- All rubber coverings at the bottom of legs of tables, stools, frames, the supporting feet of benches and the bottoms of boxes should be in place and not worn to the point where they are split or cause an imbalance.
- The rubber or plastic knobs on the top of benches, designed to absorb pressure and to stop slipping when inverted and placed on the floor for balance work, must be in place.
- Any free-standing or connecting piece that wobbles or is not otherwise firm (e.g. a ladder or plank hooked to a bar – with one end on the ground) should be investigated.
- The vinyl or leather covers on the tops of boxes, bucks, tables and stools should be intact and properly secured.
- All wooden pieces (boxes, benches, beams and bucks) should be checked for splinters, both in obvious view and underneath, and for any splits or likely splits.
- All hooks attached to the ends of benches, planks or ladders must be fully secured – one is not sufficient for safe operation – and properly covered by the prescribed material.

- All trestles must be completely stable with locking devices in full working order and properly secured.
- Mats, of whatever type and size, must be checked regularly, both for splits and slipping on the floor.

Fixed apparatus

All frames, bars and beams that have one or more sections attached to a wall must be properly secured.

- Holes for bolts must be free from dirt and fluff, allowing the bolt to enter to its full depth and the metal casing must allow the bolt top to be turned and secured.
- Wires must be intact and at the right tension.
- All locking devices must be fully operational and secure the frame properly.
- Any adjustable bars or beams must have supporting bolts or alternative locking devices that can be and are fully secured.

Improvised apparatus

When short of apparatus, it is possible to use items such as portable stage blocks, or even a small, low plinth-type stage, that are designed to be weight bearing. They must be checked rigorously, however, to ensure that they are completely stable, level and splinter-free.

- Items that are not stable, such as chairs, must never be used in gymnastics.
- If in any doubt, it is sensible to adopt a policy of not using any apparatus that has not been designed for gymnastic use.

Faulty apparatus

Any faulty piece (including 'small' apparatus) must be put out of commission immediately. The piece should either be disposed of or not used until the necessary repairs are carried out. It must be marked and secured in such a way that it would be impossible for it to be used in the interim.

- Any accident due to faulty equipment would, rightly, be laid at the door of the person who allowed it to be used.
- In some cases, it is possible to wash dirt away from the bottom of mats to restore the grip, but this must only be done if it is definitely known that the manufacturer recommends this course of action and the prescribed cleaning fluid is applied.

When in doubt – leave it out! Do not use the apparatus!

Repairs

Repairs should be undertaken only by reputable companies that specialise in gymnastic equipment.

- A specialist company may be contracted to or approved by an LEA and carry out the recommended annual inspection.
- Repairs should be carried out at the time of the inspection or very soon after a fault is identified.

Storing portable apparatus

Ideally, the apparatus should be placed round the perimeter of the hall with easy access to each separate piece or set of pieces. Where this is not possible, and pieces are blocked off in a section of the hall, the pupils should be taught to move them only when clear access to the open floor space is available. This may mean having to wait in an orderly manner until other pieces are moved.

- Each piece should always be put in the same designated place, either on specially manufactured wall brackets (e.g. ladders) or on the floor (e.g. mats or tables).
- Labels for each piece or set of apparatus can be attached to the wall, thus ensuring that teachers will always adhere to the school plan and put the pieces in the correct place.
- Trestles that easily fall over on contact should be secured to the wall using straps or clips.
- It is easier if mats are placed in two or three piles so that the distance for carrying and waiting time can be reduced and, similarly, benches placed singly or in pairs round the hall, not altogether (and *never* on top of each other!).

Setting up – positioning apparatus

All apparatus, whether being used singly or in conjunction with other pieces, must be positioned so that there are clear lines of access and space for exits from expected movements which do not directly clash with those for other apparatus sets (e.g. where it is expected that pupils may run towards a piece of apparatus or roll away on a mat).

- There must always be sufficient space between apparatus and walls and other pieces of equipment (e.g. pianos, gymnastic apparatus not being used, stage blocks) to cater for the full range of possible movements or what is being specifically practised. The gap between the two could be as much as 2 metres.
- Sensible planning in regard to both the selection and position of apparatus can help to make the activities safer. For example, boxes or tables should not be placed 'head-on' to a piano where pupils moving off may be expected to move towards it.

NB Further information on designing apparatus sets and lay-outs is included in *Designing a lay-out* and *Lay-out example for educational gymnastics* (below).

Setting up – moving apparatus

Correct lifting technique

Pupils must be taught how to carry apparatus in the correct way, gradually increasing the range and weight of what is carried as they progress through the year groups.

They should bend their knees, without stooping, take a firm grip on the apparatus and then lift keeping their backs and heads in normal alignment.

(HSC 1990)

Figure 6.1 shows the *correct* way to do this.

Figure 6.2 shows the *incorrect* way to lift, i.e. legs straight, back bent and head looking down.

The teacher can lend a great deal of assistance, particularly in the early stages, either by helping the pupils to transport or place a piece of apparatus, or by carrying and securing it alone.

Figure 6.1 Correct starting position for lifting apparatus

Figure 6.2 Incorrect starting position for lifting apparatus

Carrying mats

Mats should be carried, *never* dragged along the floor, by either two or four pupils, depending on size and age. For example,

- KS1: four pupils hold a mat at each corner. When picking the mat up or putting it down or when in a stationary position they face wholly or partially inwards. When moving, they turn their feet towards the direction of travel and walk forwards with the mat – carried lengthways – at the side of the body.
- KS2: two pupils hold a rectangular mat at the ends and, ideally, walk either sideways or half forward/sideways. One pupil walking backwards and the other forwards is *not* recommended.

Orderly queuing *at the side* of a pile of mats when they are carried out or put away leaves a clear pathway to the apparatus sets and, therefore, prevents collisions and possible injuries (see chapter 3, Figure 3.1).

Learning to set up apparatus

When learning how to set up apparatus, the pupils operate in turn.

- One group, directed and possibly assisted by the teacher, sets up apparatus and sits down when the task is completed. Another group then follows, and so on.
- As competency develops, the pupils may be allowed to move certain items concurrently (e.g. mats and benches).
- Finally, when they can be trusted to carry the items safely and avoid contact with others when doing so – *and already know precisely where it is going to be placed* – all apparatus might be got out at the same time.
- This should always be done in a calm and measured way with children taught to look out for and respect the movements of others.
- It may seem a slow process but is well worth it, both from a safety and efficiency point of view.

Lay-out

When the same lay-out is to be used for a number of lessons, it is more efficient and safer if designated groups of children always get out and put away the same pieces. The pupils rapidly learn exactly how to release (if necessary) and lift, carry and steer each piece in the set and precisely where it will be placed and secured. The same applies when the pieces are put away.

The first time a particular lay-out is set up, the teacher:

- selects groups and indicates where they should sit – in straight lines on the floor;
- shows each group *exactly* where each piece in their set goes *before* any apparatus is moved;
- depending on pupil age and experience, either assists each group in turn or allows all the groups to operate at the same time, assisting and observing as necessary.

Within a very short space of time, generally two lessons for Years 4–6, the pupils will know exactly where to put the apparatus and will move it efficiently.

If desired, it is possible to use diagrams on cards to indicate where apparatus goes.

Checking the apparatus after set-up

In every lesson where apparatus is set up, the teacher should always check each set or single item to ensure that it is safe before indicating that a group may start work.

There must never be any deviation from this rule.

- Checks should be done visually and manually, using fingers to check bolts and locking devices, and for splinters.
- On completing their setting-up tasks, pupils would normally sit down in a neat straight line, *on the floor*, adjacent to the apparatus (NB never on the apparatus).
- The teacher may then either move round all the sets in order when all setting-up is finished or respond, in turn, when each group is ready with a member informing him or her that the setting-up is complete.

Section D: Educational gymnastics

Dance and gymnastic floor work and *Apparatus*, covering basic floor activities and setting up and checking apparatus, should be read in conjunction with this section.

This type of gymnastics, in the past sometimes referred to as movement, is the type normally taught in primary schools and, in a modified form, in nursery schools. Given that tens of thousands of lessons, using a large variety of different types of apparatus, are taking place each week during term time, the low incidence of accidents is indicative of how safe this type of gymnastics is, when taught in the correct manner.

Method

The key to the excellent safety record in educational gymnastics is that tasks are normally designed so that, within limits imposed by the teacher, the *pupils select their own answers*. This is as it should be. Children are normally very aware of their own abilities and with minimal guidance will sensibly stay within their own movement capabilities.

Another important contributory factor to the low accident rate is that pupils are rarely taught specific movements and balances. This is only done when there is perceived to be a particular need (see *Task structure, Direct mode* below).

Allowing a choice of answer does not mean that accidents will *ipso facto* be prevented. Other factors of vital importance include: the teacher's general approach; the wording of tasks and how they are developed through background comment, Q and A and feedback; the design of apparatus lay-outs; the checking of apparatus for position and structural damage, and ensuring that each piece is properly secured.

Approach

Golden rule: pupils should be taught, from the outset, to behave in a calm and controlled way. If this is insisted upon, the children soon learn to accept it.

NB A low 'working' noise level or, sometimes, no noise at all, is indicative of pupil concentration on tasks, leading to high standards, and risk-free practice. This should be the norm.

Fundamentals of movement

There should be no

- over-fast or exaggerated running in any activity, nor knocking into or pushing other pupils;
- ongoing movement in a backward direction. Such movements should be controlled and limited to one phase (e.g. one jump) until pupils are capable of adding more with full control. Running or continuous jumping in a backwards direction should *never* be allowed;
- licence to simply play or move anywhere at will on any apparatus.

If pupils do not respond positively to what is expected of them or are guilty of any of the above, the lesson must be stopped and started again, until the correct response is obtained.

Safety can be compromised if pupils are allowed to dictate the lesson or ignore what they have been asked to do.

Task structure

Control, and thus safety, will be aided by properly structured tasks. Even from the earliest foundation stage, giving the pupils something to focus on works against any inclination to fool about. For example, tasks can initially be geared to moving and finishing or landing quietly, or holding a shape absolutely still in order to show how movements are controlled.

Modes

It is possible to divide gymnastic teaching and, by extension, task structuring into three modes – *indirect*, *limitation* and *direct*.

INDIRECT MODE

This mode is associated with freedom of choice. Teachers will typically issue instructions such as '*explore your apparatus*', or '*how many ways can you find?*'. As there are no specific movements or balances being asked for – the pupils choose their own – the approach is nominally safe. However, unless properly controlled, this freedom can easily lead to simply playing or fooling about and, therefore, unsafe behaviour.

LIMITATION MODE

Restrictions are imposed, based on direction, speed, body shape, body parts or modes of movement (e.g. twisting). Teachers will typically issue instructions such as '*find ways of moving with a wide body* or *sideways* or *very slowly*'. This, when coupled with target setting, for example '*find three different ways of moving sideways*', produces real concentration with, again, the pupils choosing their own answers.

A crucial point is that, when using these two modes, the teacher must phrase the task, background comments made while the children are working, advice to individuals and feedback very carefully, ensuring that there is no misunderstanding, particularly when doing apparatus work. The teacher should ALWAYS give help in the form of suggestions with, crucially, the child making the choice. For example,

'Can you (e.g. jump, take weight on your hands when you move, twist)?'

'Have you tried...?'

The teacher should NEVER make the decision for the pupils and tell them what to do or put pressure on to perform a given movement. For example,

'I want you all to jump off the apparatus.'

or directly to individuals.

'Put your hands there and throw your legs up and over.'

or seeing a pupil hesitating on a box or climbing frame.

'Come on, jump down – I know you can do it!'

Providing the environment is safe, by correctly phrasing a task, the teacher would not expect to be held responsible if an accident occurred.

There is a thin line between encouragement and coercion. Encouragement is an important element in teaching gymnastics, but coercion has no part at all.

Encouragement is recognised as the key to development in *Curriculum Guidance for the Foundation Stage* (DfEE/QCA 2000). In regard to 'Body Management', the 'practitioner' is asked to

encourage ... children to move using a range of body parts and to perform given movements at more than one speed.

(Op. cit.)

DIRECT MODE

In this command approach, the whole class or a selected group of children who have been assessed as having the *necessary capability*, may be

1   taught exactly how to execute a given movement or balance,

and at a later point in time

2   told to do it again in exactly the same way or be asked to find variations of it or to include it as part of a series of movements, possibly joined in a sequence.

The object may be to help the children progress more quickly or attain something that the majority could not do without using this method. It may be believed that it is worthwhile in its own right or it may help in developing another range of movements, such as, in the case of a handstand, ways of inverting.

Safety is often the most important factor, or an important secondary factor, in regard to both the learning and the later execution of the same or similar movements or balances. These may be relatively simple, as in the suggested two foot jumping and landing progression shown below, and therefore within the teaching capabilities of all teachers or, as with the handstand, require more specialist knowledge.

The following exercise demonstrates how a whole class may be taught to jump and land quietly and with poise on two feet, both on the floor alone and using a variety of low-level apparatus.

1   Teach either one or a number of good landing positions with feet together.
2   Jump on the spot – to land quietly and still.
3   After a limited run-up (up to three steps), land quietly and still.
4   Jump over or into or out of pieces of apparatus placed on the floor, such as hoops or ropes.
5   At a later stage, when the pupils are deemed to be capable, use objects such as benches to jump on to and off.

NB When the ability to land with good control and, therefore, safely, after jumping, has been fully developed, it can be transferred via good teaching to other types of movement.

Teacher knowledge

If a teacher hasn't received extensive instruction in gymnastics during ITT, then it is recommended that they should concentrate on floor work and using small apparatus and mats. Depending on the level of instruction received during ITT, it may also be possible to use benches.

Until help has been obtained from advisory staff and/or a suitable course taken, full apparatus sets (including portable and fixed climbing frames, boxes and tables) should not be used. There would be a serious risk of an accident and, if one occurred and litigation followed, it would be difficult to defend.

In order to teach or assist with movements and balances requiring bodily support or where a knowledge of practices and progression would be required, for example forward rolls, teachers must have covered the relevant material on a recognised course (see *Vaulting and agility* and chapters 1 and 2).

Very few such movements or balances would normally be taught in educational gymnastics lessons. However, they may have been learned in lessons devoted to gymnastic award work or in gym clubs and the pupils may wish to include them in their choice of responses to tasks set. This is perfectly acceptable and those pupils who are competent will go ahead and include them.

A problem arises, however, when pupils are only partially competent or confident and ask for assistance. Teachers MUST NOT give it, unless, as stated, they have the specialist knowledge and are confident of their ability to assist. Pupils may even sometimes tell the teacher what to do. Do not succumb. It may be tempting, given that the children are often very light, but is not worth the risk.

Specialist knowledge may be acquired on an initial teacher training PE course or in-service or other courses approved by the LEA or the school (see *Vaulting and agility* below).

Note that this advice should not stop teachers from giving minimal aid such as holding a hand to assist in a balance on a bench rib or two hands when attempting a low-level jump (e.g. from a bench, for example).

Using apparatus

Group size

Group sizes should be kept quite small. Six, seven or eight groups of four children is much better than four of seven or five of six – for both safety and achieving standards.

Small apparatus

Small apparatus can be used to augment the larger pieces and ensure that all the children can work without crowding.

Springboards

Springboards of any type should not be used in this type of gymnastics.

Designing a lay-out

It is crucially important that apparatus is positioned so that the distances between pieces are conducive to safe movement.

Figure 6.3 Apparatus – two pieces in a safe position: adjoining

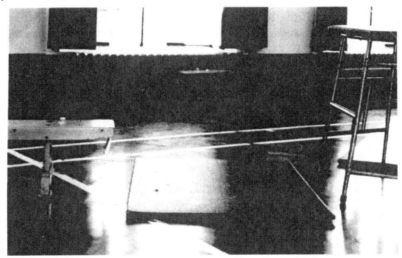

Figure 6.4 Apparatus – two pieces in a safe position: well apart with mat between

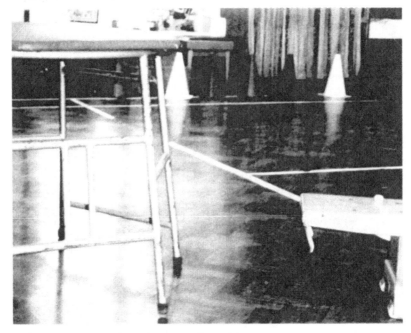

Figure 6.5 Apparatus – two pieces in an unsafe position

The pieces must be either

- so close together that it is easy to move – directly – from one to the other.
  A bench, for example, should be placed so that it is in contact, or almost in contact with other pieces (such as boxes or other benches) or partially under pieces such as bars or tables, as shown in Figure 6.3.
  or
- placed well over a metre away to allow for control to be regained after a loss of balance sustained when moving off one piece or for doing a chosen connecting movement (see Figure 6.4).

NB The pieces of apparatus should be positioned so that there is no danger of losing balance while attempting to bridge a gap, or any possibility of accidentally falling in between the two pieces and colliding with, or unintentionally landing on, one of them. Gaps that are too short, as shown in Figure 6.5, *must* be avoided.

As stated, minimal safe distances must also be left between apparatus pieces and

- fixed elements such as walls or the stage;
- moveable items such as the school piano;
- pieces of apparatus that are not being used.

The Figures 6.3 and 6.5 show cones placed round a piano, illustrating how items such as this may be cordoned off to give extra protection.

Additionally, as stated, distances between pieces in different sets of apparatus should take account of the need for adequate space between them and possible directions of movements.

Placing of mats

The most commonly asked questions on in-service courses in gymnastics is, in regard to apparatus work,

Do we need to, or should we, put mats everywhere in case the children fall?

The answer is most definitely 'no'. We do not expect the children to fall. Children are extremely good judges of their own capabilities and accidents in educational gymnastics are actually extremely rare. Providing the tasks are set correctly and the pupils behave sensibly, the chances of falling from frames, ladders or boxes are very slight indeed.

Standard one inch (2.5cm) gymnastic mats, now known by BSI as floor or foundation mats, should be placed in order to

- *indicate a point* where a controlled and intentional landing from apparatus may be executed (e.g. when coming off a table or jumping over a bench).
- *allow children to drop down comfortably* when hanging from a horizontal ladder or pole (when static or moving along). The height of the ladder or pole should be such that the dropping distance is well within the compass of all pupils.

NB In both the above cases, the mat will provide some *cushioning* to supplement the absorption of body weight by the child when carrying out a planned landing.

- *encourage pupils* to execute a movement or a combination of movements that they may not attempt if the mat was not there (e.g. to roll on to it from a squat position on the top of a bench), or follow particular pathways or find different ways of moving away from apparatus.

Placing mats indiscriminately all over the floor can, in fact, be dangerous. They may intrude into 'natural' approach routes and be the cause of tripping.

It is possible that placing mats all round the base of a climbing frame could lead to a false sense of security and encourage jumping off in a dangerous manner. It is better to use one mat (or possibly two if the frame is open on both sides) to indicate where controlled ways of dismounting may be expected, possibly leading into other movements and/or towards other pieces of apparatus.

Schools should only use mats that have been specifically manufactured for gymnastic use.

Lightweight mats, specially designed for infant use, are not suitable for landings. Use should be restricted to balances and movements where contact is maintained e.g. changing shape, rolling sideways.

Lay-out example for educational gymnastics (low to medium height level)

The lay-out in Figure 6.6 is suitable for top KS1 and lower to middle KS2.

The apparatus and mats have been deliberately positioned in order to allow for both safe distances between pieces and clear directions of approach that do not 'cross' with those used in other sets.

Arrows indicate obvious directions of approach with thin lines indicating where a run-up may be employed and the length of the actual maximum distance anticipated, but note that many other approach directions can be safely used.

There should be a 2 metre gap between any piece of apparatus, including mats, and the hall perimeter (including objects against the wall).

Set number 1

This set, based entirely on small apparatus, requires little space and is very safe. Hoops of different sizes can be used and the distance between them varied. Pupils may safely move between, in and out of a single hoop and from one to another according to the task.

The ropes can be used to move across (with or without making contact with the rope), or to follow designed patterns, or picked up and used for skipping.

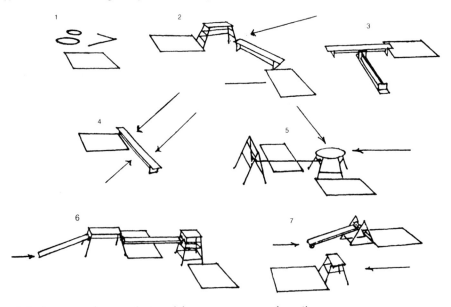

Figure 6.6 Apparatus lay-out designed for seven groups of pupils

Set number 2

The arrow shows an unimpeded run that could start from the hall perimeter. The table (2′ 6″ or 3′ / 76 cm or 91 cm) may also be approached at an angle along the bench that is in contact with the table.

The single straight rope suggests an alternative approach to the mat from the normal 'end on' approach.

Set number 3

This set, using a bench, an inverted bench rib and a mat, is designed to encourage static and dynamic balance. Greater variety and challenge can be introduced by placing bean-bags on the bench top and/or rib or laying ropes across one or both of them. Additionally, either the bags or the ropes could be placed on the floor close to one or both benches Pupils can be asked to touch them with different parts of the body, move over or pick them up as appropriate.

Set number 4

A single wooden bench gives ample provision for all four children to work *across* it doing movements that require cushioning on to the mat and those that don't on to the floor.

The bench is angled and positioned so that there is plenty of room between itself and the perimeter and a clear approach extending back between sets 2 and 5.

Set number 5

The circular table (1′ 6″ or 2′ 3″ / 46 cm or 69 cm high) can be safely approached at many different angles. The pole attached to the trestle is low and encourages movements over, under and through.

Set number 6

Very little running would be required, or expected, with the movements or balances done on the medium height (2′ or 2′ 6″ / 61 cm or 76 cm) table, wooden planks and stool, or in *transferring* from one to the next.

Set number 7

The diagram indicates safe approaches to both the low table (1′ 6″ /46 cm) and vinyl covered padded plank with positioning suggesting a circular pathway.

Note that for this lay-out:

- Mats are positioned to cushion landings on the feet (from the wooden bench, tables, stool and storming stand or small wooden trestle) and where movements on to the hands and/or into rolls (from tables and bench and over the pole) may be expected.
- Up to 28 children are catered for. In most halls, there would be room to move set 4 to the left and create another set between it and set 5 if more children have to be

catered for. Alternatively, hoops and ropes can be used separately to create another set.

- It is possible in small halls for all the sets to be moved closer together without compromising safety.

The same principles would be incorporated in all lay-outs. Variations might include two to three different sets based on wall frames with very little running involved – thus leaving ample space for approaches to the remaining sets.

Movement: directions and pathways

Normally, in order to maximise activity, children are encouraged to approach apparatus from a variety of directions. Sometimes, however, restrictions on space may mean that in order to guarantee safe movement execution, some pieces may only be approached or left using directions that have been prescribed.

Foundation and early KS1 pupils should be shown how to work as a group, sharing the pieces and learning how to take turns.

In order to avoid the possibility of collisions, very young children may be asked to follow a prescribed route. As they become accustomed to using a number of pieces, they can be gradually encouraged or allowed to use different angles of approach.

Section E: Vaulting and agility and awards

Vaulting and agility (V and A), which may also be referred to as *Formal* or *Olympic* gymnastics, involves the teaching of specific movements and balances, mainly on the floor (including mats) or a box or table. Other movements, either distinctly different or modified forms of those done on the floor or box, may be performed on bars, frames, pairs of vertical hanging ropes or benches. Many of those done on floor or box are included in gymnastic award schemes organised by British Gymnastics.

Specialist knowledge

Some movements are relatively simple. The majority, however, ranging from moderately difficult to very advanced, require knowledge not only of the actual technique but of step-by-step development, often involving other types of equipment, and, vitally, of how to give support.

A teacher must not only have covered the material required in teaching this form of gymnastics (in which pupils may often be in inverted positions) but must also feel totally confident of holding a pupil and taking the weight when necessary.

In order to teach or coach virtually all the movements and balances associated with this type of gymnastics, it is *essential* that an appropriate course, approved by the LEA or school, has been taken.

Such courses may be organised by the LEA, British Gymnastics, Higher Education institutions or other approved bodies. All British Gymnastics courses lead to a certificated qualification, with the Curricular Teachers Award being particularly appropriate for primary age teachers working at a basic level.

A teacher who has not attended an appropriate course or does not feel totally confident about supporting children should never include this type of material in lessons or assist at voluntary gym clubs where vaulting and agility, including British Gymnastics proficiency award material, is normally taught.

Pupil:teacher ratios

Only very basic low risk movements should be attempted with a whole class. Where direct teacher assistance or support is required, much smaller numbers should be taught and only in a club situation. British Gymnastics recommend a ratio of 15:1, and this should be acceptable for many movements. Where a lot of body support is required, the maximum ratio should be decreased to 10:1.

Use of mats

Basic floor movements and vaults with low momentum, or movements and vaults that do not involve inversion, can be practised and performed on a standard 1" (2.5 cm) thick floor mat *providing the children have been taught how to absorb weight on landing.* A 2" (5 cm) thick mat is recommended for vaults with greater momentum and more advanced floor movements and a 4" (10 cm) thick mat for high impact work.

Thicker weight absorbent safety mattresses (typically 8 to 12 inches (20–30 cm) in thickness) should not be used. Such mats are often known as 'crash' mats, an inappropriate description implying incorrect use. Landings are very difficult to control and it is very easy for the body to be 'thrown' in different directions on the rebound or for ankles to be turned, leading to possible muscle damage or breakages.

Teachers must be aware of the fact that a mat is designed to absorb weight on landing. It is not guaranteed to prevent injury.

Supporting or spotting pupils

Techniques for supporting (sometimes called spotting) pupils will be learned on specialist courses (see *Specialist knowledge* above). It is essential, however, that certain rules are rigidly followed when support is being given for floor and box movements.

Development

There are essentially four stages:

1. Full support – using two hands and a very firm hold on body parts as appropriate to the movement – until a stable landing position is attained.
2. Partial support – the teacher loosely holds or does not take the full weight – but is prepared to take a firm hold immediately it becomes apparent there is a need for this to be done.
3. Standing-in – not holding parts of the body but ready to take action in the event of a serious error i.e. to break a fall or catch a performer.
4. No assistance.

It is absolutely essential that progression to a subsequent stage is NOT made until the gymnast can repeatedly perform the movement being learned without error and demonstrates the confidence required to work with reduced support. If pupils make mistakes or lose confidence when working at stages 2, 3 and 4 they must go back to the preceding stage until the technique is again considered to be good and confidence is restored. The decision to progress must be a joint one between teacher and pupil, with both in full agreement. There must be no coercion.

Matting must be of the correct thickness to give the required absorbency. This may be reduced in floor work as competence grows.

Support should be automatically restored for any change in circumstances (e.g. a new environment, a box or table with a different height, shape or surface cover, or a variation asked for in the technique).

Any stress observed, such as that induced in competition, may mean, at a minimum, a return to standing-in.

Positioning

Teachers must make absolutely sure that they are in a position that provides a firm base for initial support and allows for travelling with the performer while maintaining a hold, if such movement is necessary. Particular care should be taken in regard to mats, making sure that it is possible to move on to and along them freely when required.

¤ Checklist: common pitfalls in gymnastics and dance

Potentially hazardous equipment

Trampette

This is an extremely dangerous piece of equipment. It is designed to give users a very big 'lift' in order to negotiate very high pieces of apparatus. It is not suitable for use with apparatus pieces used in primary school that are relatively low in height. Performers could either lose control through poor contact or, very often, be thrown right over the top of the apparatus, possibly sustaining very serious injuries. Even simply jumping on and off has its dangers.

It is recommended that trampettes are *not used* in primary schools.

Crash mats

Safety mattresses of the 'crash mat' type are not recommended for use in primary schools. Their good cushioning powers are offset by the lack of stability on landing.

Dangerous activities

Jumping from heights

The vast majority of pupils will correctly gauge the heights they can safely jump off climbing frames, boxes etc. A few may not.

It is recommended that pupils should be told or shown that they should not jump from heights exceeding 1 metre.

Dive forward rolls

Forward rolls should not be attempted over one or more children's bodies, nor over benches or other solid objects. Many LEAs have banned this activity in their schools.

¤ **Golden rules for safe practice in gymnastics and dance**

- *Mats should only be placed where it is expected that pupils will be attempting landings* or follow-up movements after leaving the apparatus, or to encourage movements in a particular place.
- *Mats should not be placed indiscriminately* nor simply where it is thought an accident might occur. Apparatus sets should be designed, tasks set and pupils taught so that there *is no expectation of accidents happening.*
- *Pupils should be set tasks that allow them to choose their own responses.* This is particularly important on mixed apparatus sets. Teachers should not *tell* pupils what movements to do (except when deliberately choosing to use direct teaching of movements which are deemed to be within the capabilities of ALL the pupils attempting them).
- Unless they possess the necessary specialist expertise, *teachers must never offer bodily support* to pupils aiming to improvise on apparatus or to attempt a recognised vault or agility with even a minor degree of difficulty in any type of gymnastics lesson.
- *Teachers should constantly scan the class to ensure that all pupils are working sensibly.* Comments can be made from the perimeter looking in, thus allowing the teacher to constantly observe the whole class as they work. Teachers can move in to offer help to groups or individuals, but they should still make regular checks on the rest of the class.
- *Apparatus must be positioned safely.* Adjacent pieces should be either so close together that safe transfer can be made, or far apart so that there is no possibility of colliding with one after an error in execution on another.
- *Children should be taught how to carry and set up apparatus safely*, gradually attempting more with increasing strength and experience.
- *All apparatus must be in a good state of repair and thoroughly checked before use.*
- *An annual inspection of all equipment should be carried out* and any necessary repairs either undertaken at the time or as soon afterwards as is possible.
- *Faulty equipment should be taken out of use immediately* and either repaired or disposed of.

7   Small apparatus work

Small apparatus embraces beanbags, balls ranging in size from small to medium, flat wooden or plastic playbats, canes, loose ropes and quoits. The wide range of activities possible with these pieces can be seen as leading into or as part of games, gymnastics or athletics, or as activities in their own right.

Some basic activities such as balancing a beanbag on different body parts while remaining on the spot or moving in and out of a hoop on the floor may be safely done in a school hall. The majority of activities, however, particularly where objects are being thrown, passed or struck or where a reasonable amount of space is needed for pupils to move into new positions or intermingle freely, must be done on a playground, field, or, when available, a large sports hall.

All class members may work with the same piece or the class may be divided into halves, thirds or, in the later stages of development, groups of four working on different activities.

As with games and athletics, cones, skittles and marker domes can be used for activities and to delineate operational areas.

Checking

Wooden apparatus

Pieces made of wood must be checked for splinters and splitting. Canes are prone to split at the ends and they should be taped when new for use in jumping activities. Taping will also help to prevent them sliding rapidly over indoor floors. If any wooden hoops are still in stock, taping at three equidistant points will help to protect them and to hold them in position on smooth floors.

Handles of wooden playbats must be intact and firm in order to give a proper grip. If one of the two shaped wooden pieces that may be attached to the handle core has come off or is loose, it must be properly attached again. If this is not possible or the piece is too worn, the bat must be replaced.

NB It is not safe to use a bat with just one piece in place or so worn that the shape has been lost.

Plastic hoops

Plastic hoops must be perfectly round. If broken, they must be disposed of.

Beanbags

Beanbags must not be worn or split at the stitching.

Skipping ropes

Skipping ropes must be in good condition and repaired or replaced if they begin to split at the ends or the centre.

¤ **Collecting and returning (NB Storage is covered in chapter 3)**

Classes should be organised into four house, animal or, simply, colour groups.

One small ball, beanbag and skipping rope for each child in the group plus other items depending on age (e.g. longer rope, soft balls, some quoits, airflow balls and bats) should be placed in each of four storage baskets, all designated with a band of the appropriate colour. It is helpful if compartmentalised baskets are used.

It can also be helpful if hoops are either tied together in sets using a coloured band, the number and size reflecting the age of the children, or placed on the pegs provided on specially designed stands or wheeled trolleys. Larger balls should be placed in separate baskets or sacks. If more playbats are required, it is safer if they are carried out in separate baskets.

Pupils should be designated to carry or, if on a trolley, wheel the baskets to four different dispersal/collection points (well clear of any wall or similar hazard).

The class should then line up on command facing the basket and at right angles to, not in, the area where the activity is to take place (see Figure 7.1).

The children then take what is required from their 'team' distribution point to the place designated for practice.

Carrying and placing apparatus

NB The apparatus must *always be carried*, and never thrown, hit or rolled.

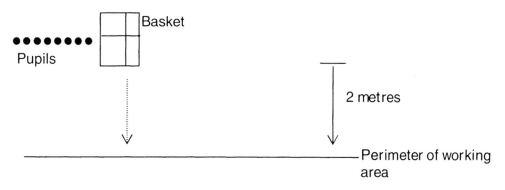

Figure 7.1 Distribution of small apparatus from containers

- On completion of the practice, the apparatus should be carried back to the collection point and *placed* in the basket, sack or other container, or at a given point as specified.
- Allowing pieces to be thrown, hit, kicked or propelled in any other way towards the collection point may create danger, with pupils tripping or being hit. It may also lead to problems in the future regarding attitude towards good order and, in turn, safety.

Leaving equipment lying about after use, either in or adjacent to the area being used for the activity, can be very dangerous – it is very easy to turn an ankle on a ball or trip over a bat. Similarly, baskets, sacks or other containers must always be placed out of the 'action zone' where the children are working.

If the pupils are to work in parallel on different activities, the groups should be set up and positioned and the activities explained before the equipment is collected.

Starting work

According to instructions, pupils will either:

- begin work, or set up equipment to do so, immediately the items have been collected; or
- stand, crouch or sit while holding – but not playing with – the pieces of equipment, or place the pieces on the floor and wait for a signal to begin or for further instructions.

Running and jumping activities with canes, laths or hoops

If the object is to run or jump over or into (as appropriate) canes, laths or hoops, then the apparatus must never be tied to objects (e.g. posts or skittles).

If a cane is placed in the grooves of a wire skittle, pupils must never attempt to jump or run over from the wrong direction i.e. from the side where the cane is positioned.

- It should be noted that a number of physical educationalists believe that canes or laths should only be used if the ends are further protected by additional padding, such as corks, or are constructed in the manner of dumbbells, to prevent any possibility of them causing a wound.

Organisation and development

Working alone

When pupils are working on their own, there must be sufficient *personal space* for any given activity to be done safely. For example,

- as stated, activities such as moving in and out of a hoop and balancing a beanbag may be possible indoors, but throwing and catching with an emphasis on increasing height (requiring a working circle of up to 6 metres) may have to be done on a playground or field;

- a lot of space would also be required for activities where pupils move in and out of each other, for example controlling a ball in some way or bowling a hoop;
- if there is any danger of crossing, pupils should work in turn (e.g. 'A's followed by 'B's).

Working in pairs

Pairs may work in selected areas of the playground, field or, very occasionally, the hall either *freely* or in prescribed *'formations'* according to the nature of the activity.

For example, skipping, using one or two ropes, and hoop work may be done either on the spot or by moving freely between other pairs, depending on the activity.

The throwing and catching of beanbags, balls and quoits and propelling or returning a ball using other parts of the body (e.g. the feet) or bats or racquets requires a sensible pattern of pupils standing in lines if the activities are to be safe.

- As such activities may often require participants to move backwards or chase after balls that have been missed, it is very important that there is sufficient clear space behind each pair to either remove the possibility of colliding altogether or reduce the chances very considerably.
- There must also be adequate distance between each pair to reduce any possibility of being hit by another pair's ball. This would vary according to the activity, being around 2–3 metres for straight throwing and catching, and 5 metres when using a bat.
- The best system is to have one single line of pairs stretching down the playground. If the area is not long enough, there should be a gap of at least 5 metres, but preferably 10 metres or more, between sets of pairs, depending on the activity (see Figure 7.2).

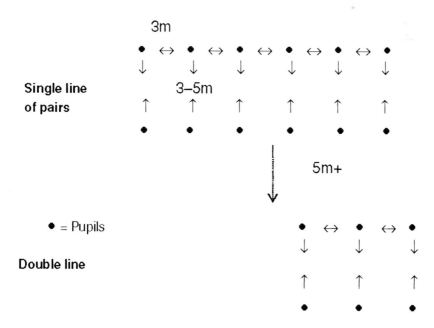

Figure 7.2 Formations for single or double lines of paired pupils

Group work

Group work means that different sections of the class are working on different activities, sometimes using the same apparatus but, more normally, a wide range of different pieces. If organised properly, with due regard to spacing and direction, it can be a very safe way of letting the class experience many varied activities in one or more lessons and/or differentiating on the basis of ability. Groups can range from half the class to sets of four children.

The principles of group work are outlined in Appendix C.

Progression

It is strongly recommended that beanbags should be used initially in throwing, catching and target work, both when operating alone and in larger units, and a high degree of competence in these skills achieved before progressing to small balls. This will ensure that the potentially dangerous rolling and bouncing of the balls in different directions across the playground when they are first introduced, often due to dropped catches and poor throwing control, will be kept to a minimum.

8 Games

This chapter is divided into sections as follows:

A   General principles for games
B   Invasion games
C   Striking and fielding games
D   Net games.

A summary of the most important safety points for all types of games is included at the end of this chapter.

Section A: General principles for games

Most games fall into the categories of *Invasion*, *Striking and Fielding* and *Net*. They may, according to their nature, involve practices done individually, in pairs or in larger groups.

There are also simple competitive chasing activities and relays that may, usually in a modified form, involve some of the ball skills employed in invasion and striking and fielding games. Both of these are covered in chapter 9.

Small-sided games and group practices

When Invasion and Striking and Fielding varieties are played, it would be expected that they would normally be small-sided or scaled down versions of the 'full' game (e.g. four-a-side soccer, mini-basketball, or *rota* cricket or rounders with, say, 4–8 players rotating between striking, bowling and fielding).

NB This allows for maximum participation as well as much greater opportunity to play at an individual's ability level (*'differentiation'*).

Such game forms and group practices, many of which replicate game situations, are a little more difficult to organise and more consideration may have to be given to safety factors. The end product, however, more than justifies the effort. Therefore, the temptation to play large side games because they are simpler to organise, allow easy observation of all the players and because the children often want to play them, should be avoided.

Small side and solo and pairs games and differentiated group practices, set up to match pupil ability, are suited to the children's needs and can be organised so that there is a minimum of risk.

Surfaces

Surfaces are vitally important. They should be suited to the activities, always in good condition and thoroughly checked before use. (Full details in regard to fields, playgrounds and synthetic surfaces are given in chapter 3, *Surfaces*.)

Clothing and footwear

Footwear should provide the grip necessary for the conditions. Wet grass is dangerous and it must be ensured that the pupils are wearing trainers with soles or boots with studs that will allow the necessary hold.

As with all PE activities, clothing should be appropriate for the activity and weather conditions, hair should be secured and jewellery removed (see chapter 2).

NB It is most important that, as most game activities are played outside, the pupils are warm enough. Being even slightly cold can lead to lack of concentration that, in turn, can mean a greater possibility of things going wrong.

Equipment

All balls, hitting implements, markers, portable posts, goals and other equipment should be carried with great care. (For distribution methods for small items see chapter 7.)

Pupils must never be allowed to carry just a single ball or hitting implement. It is obviously very tempting to throw or kick balls to space, or to or at fellow class members, or to poke or pat them with a bat. All balls should be carried in sacks, baskets or boxes as appropriate.

Large or heavy portable equipment

Special care must be taken with large and/or heavy portable pieces of equipment such as netball or badminton posts or small goals.

Transporting such pieces should be directly supervised by a teacher.

When the apparatus is too heavy for the pupils to handle alone, hands-on assistance should be given by an adult. (NB It is sometimes possible to have such equipment set up in advance by an authorised adult e.g. the caretaker. When this is done, it should still be checked before use.)

Separate posts must be bona fide products with bases designed to ensure that they will not fall over if contact is accidentally made with them.

Posts and goals

All posts and goals, whether portable or permanent, and other fixed apparatus should be in good condition and *totally secure*. For example, there must be no possibility of a cross bar breaking and posts falling down. All should be regularly inspected for cracks, sharp edges or movement. If there are any problems, remedial action must be taken immediately or the equipment taken out of use until it can be properly repaired or replaced. No chances should be taken. Nets must be properly secured and should not extend beyond the area delineated by the base of the posts.

NB In recent years, there have been a number of fatalities caused by goalposts that were unsafe. In recognition of the high level of danger associated with this piece of apparatus, the *Football Association's Goalpost Safety Guidelines* are reprinted in full in Appendix D. Although designed for soccer, many of the points made apply to goals used in other games.

Improvising

Portable posts designed for other purposes, such as those used in netball, should never be connected by a rope for use as a goal or in bat or racquet activities. Contact with the rope can pull the posts over in an inward direction leading to possible injury. Similarly, nets should only be attached to posts designed for the purpose, such as those used in badminton.

It is possible to safely improvise small goals by placing a protected cane or lath on top of cones or skittles.

Only equipment manufactured to the appropriate European or British Standard should be used.

Positioning of playing areas

The siting of pitches and practice areas is vitally important. At least 2 metres should be left between the perimeter lines of a pitch or the outer limit of a practice area and any object or surface condition that may lead to possible injury on contact. Walls, fences, posts or other objects embedded in the ground, any protruding object, portable objects, piles of rubbish that cannot be moved, loose grit and surface holes would all come in this category.

Where there are unprotected windows, activities using 'normal' game balls should take place a considerable distance away. Modified or alternative games using soft sponge or airflow balls may be played closer to the building in question.

Proximity of roads or other buildings, including residential, must be taken into account when planning games lessons. Practice and play should either take place at a distance where balls would not be expected to reach these areas or be organised in such a way (via equipment or conditioning) that the activity is safe.

Direction of play

Practices or small-sided games that involve the striking (e.g. hitting or kicking) or throwing of balls in a given direction should be organised in such a way and/or with sufficient distance between each activity to remove the risk of other group or game members being hit and players colliding when fielding balls. Details of how to set up different types of activity safely are given in the sections on invasion and striking and fielding games (*Playing areas and conditions*, *Siting* and *Direction of play*) below and in Appendix C, *Group work*.

Section B: Invasion games

Invasion games are those in which players intermingle i.e. 'invade' each other's territory. They include:

- mini-basketball (a version created for primary age children);
- rugby (league and union);
- netball;

- soccer;
- hockey and Unihoc (a version designed for KS2 pupils).

They also include a host of small-sided hand passing games using balls of different types and sizes, quoits or other small pieces of equipment, that are particularly suited to KS2 pupils.

¤ *Contact*

Particular care must be exercised in the playing of versions of games such as soccer or rugby where body contact may be allowed or expected.

Great caution should also be taken if *practices* are set up to develop techniques such as tackling where contact is allowed.

- Pupils should be matched for both size and aptitude.
- Care should be taken over the nature and descriptions of the practices to ensure that the actions required cannot be misconstrued.
- The correct skill and angles of approach should be shown and explained and pupil understanding checked before one-on-one or group practices are set up.
- In developing the skill in game-related practices, it is recommended that tackling is *encouraged* rather than *insisted* upon.

In regard to rugby, to be totally safe it is recommended that mini versions are played that specifically exclude tackling and scrums where any forward pressure is applied.

Games where tackling is expected, such as soccer, must not be played on hard surfaces. Such surfaces include concrete, tarmac and grassed surfaces, possibly with bare patches, that have become very hard in hot weather or icy conditions.

NB If hard surfaces are to be used, the games should be 'conditioned' so that tackling and other body contact (e.g. shoulder charging) are not allowed.

¤ *Teacher participation*

Teachers should *never* take part in a game where body contact is allowed or may occur. It is advisable that teachers *do not participate in any invasion game*, as even unintended contact (possibly caused through not seeing a pupil or loss of balance) can easily lead to pupil injury.

Teachers can participate *in a limited capacity* in practices and small side games, e.g. to demonstrate positional play or movement after making a pass – as opposed to ongoing play.

Playing areas and conditions

The size of pitches and practice areas, as well as goals, posts and other equipment, should match the needs of the pupils. There should be ample room to participate safely but young children should not be expected to play using dimensions designed for adults or secondary pupils.

Practice areas or mini-pitches should be clearly defined. This can be done by

* using *lines*, possibly of different colours, either permanently painted on a playground or synthetic surface (see Appendix B) or using non-toxic materials – not creosote – on a grassed surface

and/or

* placing *markers* on corners and, if necessary, along side or end lines.

  ○ The markers must be pieces of equipment designed for the purpose and which will not, in themselves, present any danger.
  ○ The best are *cones* (easily visible on any surface) and *marker domes* (small and light and very easy to place and collect).
  ○ A combination of cones on corners and domes to highlight lines is ideal (see Figure 8.1).

Figure 8.1 A ball passing game played on a court marked by cones, domes and lines

  ○ *Wire skittles* may be used as alternatives to cones and, if short of markers, beanbags, when they will be clearly visible (e.g. playground or short grass).
  ○ *Corner flags*, if manufactured for the purpose and properly secured, may also be used. They should be high, have a rounded top and be pliable enough to ensure that movement away occurs on contact. This is to ensure that there is no danger of hitting the top of the post causing damage to and possible piercing of the body.
  ○ Objects not designed for the purpose, such as cricket stumps, poles, boxes, equipment baskets or chairs, should never be used as markers.
  ○ *Always use markers manufactured for the purpose in order to ensure safety!*

When working in small groups, the grid system of marked squares or rectangles, as illustrated in Figure 8.2, can be used for practices.

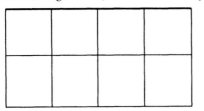

Figure 8.2 A basic grid

Practices and small-sided or overload games (e.g. 3 vs 1) can be made even safer if demarcation lines are not common to two or more activities, as shown in Figure 8.3.

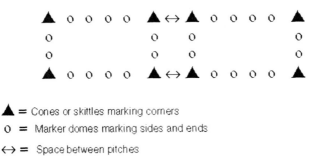

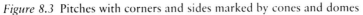

▲ = Cones or skittles marking corners

o = Marker domes marking sides and ends

↔ = Space between pitches

Figure 8.3 Pitches with corners and sides marked by cones and domes

Positioning of playing areas

The siting of pitches and practice areas is very important. As stated, a spacing of at least two metres must be allowed between the outer limit of pitches and practice areas and any object or surface that is likely to cause harm on contact (in some cases, it may also be necessary to leave such a space *between* the pitches and practice areas).

For detailed coverage of the siting of pitches and practice areas see *General principles for games, Positioning of playing areas* above.

Safe practice in specific invasion games

NB General points on safety applying to all invasion games are covered in the general and basic invasion games sections above.

All hand passing games

The following quotation from *Mini-Basketball Guidelines* (see Appendix F) applies to all games of this type

> A player shall not block, hold, push, charge, trip, impede the progress of an opponent by extending his arm, shoulder, hip or knee ... nor use rough tactics.
>
> (Mini-Basketball England)

NB Finger nails should be short

Association Football ('Soccer')

FOOTWEAR

Ideally, studded footwear should be worn on grass (the FA recommend from Year 5). Studs should be checked regularly for sharp edges and pupils should not be allowed to play in boots if the studs do not reach the required standard. Studs must always be used on *wet* grass!

It is recommended that shin pads should be worn when studded footwear is in use.

GOAL POSTS

See *General principles for games, Equipment* above. Full notice should be taken of the *Goalpost Safety Guidelines* detailed in Appendix D.

BALLS

Size 3 balls are recommended for KS3 and 4, and size 4 balls for KS5 and 6. These sizes should never be exceeded. Heavier balls are more difficult to kick and goalkeepers are very prone to broken wrists when they are used.

Basketball (mini)

Only *mini-basketball*, a version of the game which has been specially designed for the upper primary school age range, should be played. Basketball itself, with its heavy ball, large court size and overly high ring, is not only unsuitable but dangerous. It is recommended that mini-basketball and its related practices should only be played by pupils in Years 5 and 6.

When, as would normally be the case, the game is played outdoors, the posts with backboard attached should be cemented into the ground and all fittings regularly checked.

Hockey/Unihoc

It is recommended that modified versions of hockey or Unihoc, using a specially designed plastic stick and a special plastic or rubber ball, should be played. The stick is light and pliable and if contact is made accidentally the danger of injury is minimal, much less than if a wooden stick was being used. The blade being large makes it easier to make contact with whatever ball is being used and to exercise good control.

Pitches should be smooth and level, and all goals should be in good condition and fully secured (see Appendix D).

ADAPTED GAMES

Versions of the game that are non-contact and limit back swing are ideal for KS2. For example, 'Push' hockey – the stick is kept in contact with the ground when in possession and the ball 'pushed' to make a pass. This can be developed so that the stick is lifted gently – limited at the extreme to knee height. As well as a specially designed ball, 'Push' hockey may be played with a beanbag, a quoit or a puck, all of which, by design, encourage contact with the ground, or a 3–4″ (7–10 cm) hollow rubber ball.

HOCKEY BALLS

If actual hockey sticks are used, soft or 'pudding' balls are much safer than the true hard hockey ball. On playgrounds, only soft or pudding balls should be used.

HOCKEY STICKS

Sticks must be in good condition. They must not be used if splintered or broken.

PROTECTION IN HOCKEY

In hard ball versions:

- shin pads are recommended;
- goalkeepers should wear body armour, pads, kickers, gloves and a helmet plus mask.

Mouth guards are recommended for all games using a hard ball and/or all versions of the game other than those based on pushing the ball.

Netball

Post bases should be of sufficient weight to ensure stability and should not project on to the court.

Pop-Lacrosse

This is a safe version of lacrosse developed for KS2. It is played with plastic sticks, a special light pop-lacrosse or soft rubber ball and an unprotected goal. Contact is not allowed.

- The goal may be an actual lacrosse goal or a large hoop (supported in a position between the vertical and an outward lean of 45 degrees).
- The game can be made safer still by eliminating close marking and stressing interception and scooping from the ground as the ways to gain possession.

Rugby (League and Union)

The points made above regarding tackling and body contact and pitch markings are vitally important.

As stated, it is strongly recommended that mini versions that do not embrace tackling and true scrummaging should be taught.

New Image Rugby is excellent in regard to concept and safety.

- A two-handed touch (one on each hip) is used instead of a tackle, with players having to release the ball when contact is made.

- There are versions of the games suited to KS2 with teams ranging in numbers from 4 to 9. The stress, initially, should be on the smaller sided games, particularly 4 and 5.
- Players may take up the scrum front row positions in order to experience the 'feel' in the 7–9-a-side versions but there should be no pushing at any point. NB Hookers are allowed to 'hook' the ball back unimpeded, according to put-in (see Figure 8.4)
- In the 3- or 4-a-side versions, there are 2 or 3 backs and just one forward who can either hook or use a Rugby League type play-the-ball (see Figure 8.5)

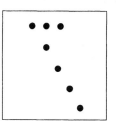

Figure 8.4 New Image Rugby – seven-a-side line-up (three forwards, four backs)

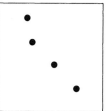

Figure 8.5 New Image Rugby – four-a-side line-up (one forward, three backs)

SURFACES

Although practices involving passing may be undertaken on playgrounds, the game should be played on grass, given that a two-handed touch may unintentionally lead to a player losing balance and falling over.

TACKLING

If rugby with tackling is to be played, then

- posts should be padded to a height of 2 metres;
- mouth guards should be worn.

Disabled pupils

Special care must be taken to ensure that

- visually impaired or hard of hearing/deaf pupils participating in a game are able to receive signals and follow the ball etc. in flight;
- surface conditions are suitable for anyone in a wheelchair or with limited mobility.

Section C: Striking and fielding games

Striking and fielding games suitable for playing in primary schools in full and/or scaled down or conditioned versions include the well-known cricket and rounders plus softball, stoolball and longball. There are also many other lesser-known games based on the principle of hitting or propelling a ball in some way and running round or between a number of markers.

The balls in the 'adult' versions of such games may be very hard (cricket) or quite hard (rounders, stoolball, softball). As such, unless full precautions are taken, there is the potential for danger in their use. When these balls are used, in the case of cricket and, possibly, softball, protective clothing would be necessary in given roles and in these, and other games, minimum fielding distances in front of the bat may be specified.

NB The key is to use softer balls in the development of the activities and, possibly, in all versions of the game that are played in the school. For example, tennis balls may be used for practices and games of cricket, rounders and stoolball.

Teacher participation

Teachers should not play in matches as members of a team or in solo rotation type activities. As batsmen, the power generated in a shot or hit and, as bowlers, the speed of delivery, even if 'controlled', could lead to serious injury; in fielding, there is the danger of collisions and knocking pupils over.

The 'active' role should be limited to demonstrations. These may be in the context of the game situation but the action would be pre-ordained and never at full power.

Siting

Given the possible hardness of the balls and the distances they may be hit, extra-special care must be taken over the boundaries and direction of play. For example, there would be absolutely no defence in law if a ball went through a driver's windscreen or struck a pedestrian from hits made from a game or practice sited close to a road or public pathway.

Direction of play

Practices or small side games that involve the striking or throwing of balls in a given direction should be organised in such a way and with sufficient distance between each activity to minimise the risk of other group members being hit or players colliding when fielding balls.

This may be done by working either *in parallel*, or *outwards* from a common central point.

In parallel

Figure 8.6 shows the best system, striking in two different directions.

The system provides for:

* a large space between groups hitting in the same direction;
* a 'free' area behind each group that allows practices and solo games to be played; without a player standing behind the striker.

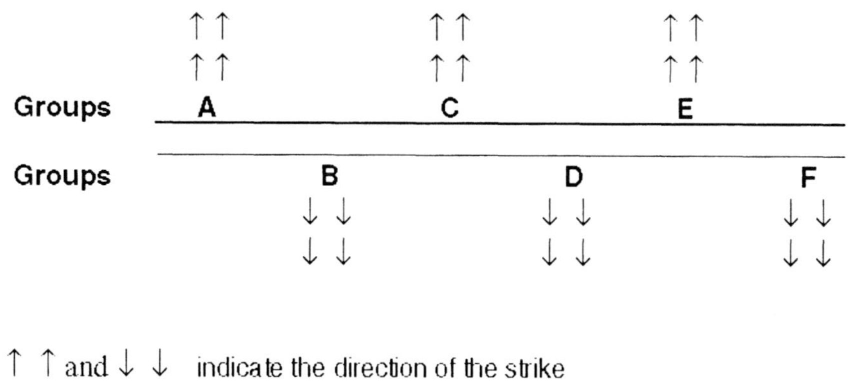

Groups   A   C   E

↑ ↑   ↑ ↑   ↑ ↑
↑ ↑   ↑ ↑   ↑ ↑

Groups   B   D   F

↓ ↓   ↓ ↓   ↓ ↓
↓ ↓   ↓ ↓   ↓ ↓

↑ ↑ and ↓ ↓ indicate the direction of the strike

Figure 8.6 Group work: striking in parallel – in alternate directions

If there is limited space, all groups must work in one direction, with groups closer together.

Outwards

This system has pupils striking from a central 'square' or 'hexagon' depending on the number of groups (see Figure 8.7).

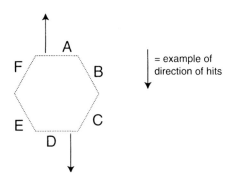

= example of direction of hits

Figure 8.7 Group work – striking outwards from a hexagon

NB The dotted lines would not normally be marked.

- Cones are placed at corners.
- The strikers A, B, C, D, E, F must hit *forwards* from a point designated by stumps or skittles in cricket or hoops in rounders type games and practices (strikers stand alongside the hoop with the ball passing over it).

Target areas

The activities can be made even safer by further reducing the possibility of fielders colliding. Each striker must aim to hit or roll the ball etc. into a very limited target area (see Figure 8.8 overleaf).

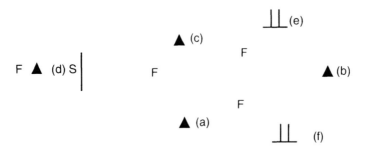

Figure 8.8 Targeted striking

The above may be set up for a striking practice or a solo competition operating in groups of 4 or 5. In each case the striker S aims to direct the ball through the markers (a) and (c). In the practice, he or she attempts to drive the ball between the markers (e) and (f), in the competition, to run round all the markers (a, b, c and d) before the fielders F retrieve the ball and either return it to any cone ahead of the runner or pass it a specified number of times.

Readiness for play

No ball should be bowled, pitched or thrown to a player in any game or related practice until it is seen that he or she is ready and fielders are facing the striker.

NB Pupils should be taught to check for themselves before delivering a ball in a group game or practice situation.

No member of a batting team waiting a turn to bat should be so close that there is a danger of being hit by bat or ball. Waiting areas should be delineated in some way.

NB An example is given in Figure 8.9 (below).

Equipment

Every piece of equipment should be thoroughly and regularly checked.

Bats

- Bats must never be split nor chipped to the point where ball flight may be affected on contact. They should, where appropriate, be bound or, otherwise, replaced.
- Handle grips, where required, must always be in top-class condition. They should be replaced or repaired as soon as signs of wear appear.
- Bats should be of an appropriate size and weight for those participating.

Pads

- Pads must not be split or have any fasteners missing.
- The actual 'padding' should always be in position and in such a condition that full protection is offered.
- Pads should be of an appropriate size and type for the activity.

Gloves or mitts

- Gloves and mitts, as manufactured for the purpose and fully intact, should be worn by wicket keepers in cricket or the catcher in softball when hard balls are used.

Cricket

Equipment for cricket

STUMPS

It is recommended that when the item is not included as part of a set, as in Kwik Cricket, *spring back or weighted base stumps* are used. There are no exposed points and the sets may be used on any surface. They have the added advantage of being easy to put into position.

When *'real' stumps* with sharp metal points are used, care must be exercised with transportation and placement.

BATS

Bats should be matched in size and weight to the pupils. They should never be thrown towards other players or stumps or on to the ground.

Soft ball versions

These use a variety of balls and offer an excellent introduction to the skills and, in modified form, the game of cricket.

Given that the vast majority of schools do not have a grass area or synthetic surface that is safe to play on with a hard ball, using a tennis, rubber or plastic ball may be the only safe option.

For many pupils, who may be afraid of a hard ball, these options offer not only a safe but, possibly, a better confidence building introduction to the game.

KWIK CRICKET

This version uses only plastic equipment and allows for a very safe initial development of the game. As the ball is so light and cannot be hit very far, a quite small overall playing area will suffice and the practices and small group games can be played reasonably close together.

ROTA(TIONAL) CRICKET

This may take the form of a competitive practice or game, either solo or in pairs. Players (working in groups of 6–8) all take part with one or two batting and bowling and the others fielding, all rotating after two or more overs. Different types of balls can be used, with tennis or medium soft rubber the safest.

SEMI-HARD BALL

There are now balls available which cover the whole hardness range between tennis and leather balls. All have a degree of 'give', with some having a seam, and offer a very good alternative to moving straight on to hard balls. They can be used in small group practices and games, provided the playing surface is suitable and even. Protective clothing should still be worn with many of them.

Hard ball

Games, such as the *rota* types described above, may be conditioned or practices set up so that it is safe to use medium to hard balls. The balls are either lobbed up underarm or bounced from the hand in front of the chest. Practices may be limited to certain types of shot.

Using conditioned practices can be seen as a safer way of introducing a harder ball to children.

THE WICKET

A hard ball can only be bowled where either a prepared grass or a specially manufactured synthetic wicket is available.

- A grass wicket must be level, regularly cut and free from holes therefore providing a reasonably even bounce.
- A synthetic wicket must be free from damage and splits and either permanently in place or secure and flat when positioned.
- It would be highly dangerous to attempt to bowl on surfaces that do not match up to these standards and, also, in inappropriate weather conditions (surface too wet and slippery or too hard and cracked).

THE BALL

The ball must be of the correct size and weight (max. 4¼ ounces/135 gm) for KS2 pupils.

PROTECTIVE CLOTHING

Appropriate protective clothing, as stated, and, also, footwear (boots or trainers with a good grip) must be worn.

HELMETS

The English Cricket Board (ECB) guidance for young players states

> Players should regard a helmet **with a faceguard** as a normal item of protective equipment and a young player should not be allowed to bat or to stand up to the stumps when keeping wicket without a helmet against a hard ball <u>except with parental permission</u>.

(ECB)

It is strongly recommended that, when a hard leather or composition ball is being used, all pupils when batting or keeping wicket in a position close to the stumps – in practice or matches – should wear a helmet (conforming to BS7928:1998). Although the ECB suggests that a child may take part without wearing a helmet, providing he or she has parental permission, a teacher should not necessarily be prepared to operate on those terms. If the teacher believes that the wearing of helmets is an essential aid to preventing serious injuries then *all* children taking part should wear them when batting or keeping wicket. It is also worth considering that, in an action alleging negligence, the parental disclaimer may not carry much weight in a court of law.

FIELDING AND WICKET KEEPING – DISTANCES

The ECB and the English Schools' Cricket Association have recommended that all fielders, other than the wicket keeper, under the age of 13, must be at least 11 yards (10 m) from the bat, except behind the wicket on the off side. Lines or markers may be used to show this distance from the batting crease.

Fielders may advance from their positions when a ball has been hit in order to catch or field it.

Wicket keepers may be close enough to catch a ball before the second bounce but not so there is any danger of being hit by the bat.

NB It is strongly recommended that all schools follow these guidelines.

GAME AND PRACTICE LAY-OUT

Additional care should be taken when setting up games and practices using a hard ball. Ideally all games etc. should either radiate outwards or be played in parallel as shown in Figure 8.6. If in parallel, there should be sufficient distance between each game or practice to ensure that a ball from one does not enter the fielding area of another.

To make the activity safer

- restrictions on types of shot may be imposed; and/or
- limitations may be imposed in regard to the hitting arc (see *Direction of play, Outwards* above).

Summary

It is recommended that cricket using a hard ball should only be played if:

- The teacher has good knowledge of the game and the possible dangers, preferably having taken a national award or attended an LEA course.
- The skills have been progressively developed, initially using a soft ball, and the pupils are fully aware of the restrictions imposed, the need for protection and the correct procedure. The children must be mature enough and deemed to be capable of playing, safely, with such a ball.
- The operating conditions are totally safe and the pupils are wearing the necessary protective gear.

Rounders

A variety of games based on rounders may be played. The common factor is that strikers, after propelling a ball, normally forwards, often but not always using a stick or bat, will aim to run round a number of base markers, either in one attempt or in stages. Four, five or six markers can be laid out as a circle, semi-circle, diamond or rectangle.

- The modified semi-circle with gradually reducing base distances shown in Figure 8.9 is excellent for games where each player in a team has one attempt to get round and scores one point for each base passed.
- It is recommended that batters should not be asked to turn through less than a right angle at any marker.

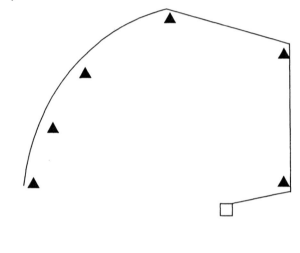

Figure 8.9 Modified semi-circular pitch for rounders-type games

Markers

A number of different objects may be safely used.

- *Hoops* – on grass only. The advantage is that they are easily put in position and adjusted. Strikers may be asked to run round them or to put one foot in when passing or stopping. Hoops should not be used on harder, smoother surfaces where they are inclined to slide on contact with feet.
- *Cones* – on all surfaces. Pupils may be asked to run round and, possibly, touch them with a stick.
- *Rounders posts and bases.* The sticks must be smooth and rounded at the top.
- Cricket stumps or pointed sticks must never be used.

Sticks and bats

Sticks and bats should be carried round by the striker. It is extremely dangerous to allow pupils to drop the stick after completing a strike. In the excitement the stick can end up being thrown backwards and cause injury to anyone fielding behind the striker.

In the event of a school having insufficient sticks or bats, it is advised that sufficient are purchased as soon as possible. In the meantime, the bats may be put in a hoop stationed to the side and slightly behind the striker. The stick or bat *must* be *placed* in the receptacle in order for points or rounders to be scored.

NB It should be stressed from the outset, and pupils constantly reminded, that *striking implements should never be thrown.*

Balls

The regulation rounders ball is quite hard and also quite small. There is some danger of the ball being missed in fielding and causing injury. It is recommended that children develop the skills involved using softer, larger balls (e.g. a fairly soft rubber ball and/or a tennis ball). Some children will make more progress and be better protected if such balls are always used.

Fielding

It is recommended that children stand a minimum distance of 10 metres in front of the bat and 5 metres behind.

Batting team base

It is most important that members of a batting team who are waiting their turn to bat remain well out of the active playing area. The area should be cordoned off, using cones. It is recommended that this area is positioned to the left of the last base and at least 5 metres away (see Figure 8.9).

Matching to age

Young pupils using regulation rounders sticks and balls very often fail to make contact. It is recommended that pupils are only ever allowed to attempt the full game in the later stages of KS2 and that only after a step-by-step development using, say, playbats and larger balls. It may also be better if rounders 'bats' (shaped like a miniature cricket bat) are used, as opposed to thin sticks.

Versions of rounders where one or more soft balls are projected forwards and the fielding team must complete a task, such as returning all balls to a bin before the striker can run round the markers, are strongly recommended. As they are very safe and allow for a lot of activity on each throw, they are particularly suitable for younger KS2 and inexperienced children. (For example, balls may be rolled, bounced, kicked or struck from the hand by a bat and the fielders may roll, bounce or throw them to other team members or, even line up and roll or pass the ball between all pairs of legs.)

Softball

Only pupils who have undergone a full progression of striking and bowling practices and have the necessary strength and co-ordination should attempt this game.

To play a proper game a regulation pitch should be marked out on the grass. However, diamonds or other shaped pitches, with different distances between the bases, can be created using large hoops instead of marked boxes. Recommended inter-base distances should not be exceeded (see Softball in Appendix F).

Development

As with other striking games, tennis balls may be used when introducing the game. In many respects, however, larger balls are more suited to the softball bat. Specially manufactured 'safety' balls can be used for practice and the regulation softball for games. Smaller harder balls such as for rounders or stoolball should not be used.

Pitching

It is recommended that what is termed *slow pitch* should be used. The ball must be thrown underarm, from a minimum distance of 11 metres up to Year 5 or 12 metres for Year 6, using a lob action with a definite arc (2–4 metres in a match). The ball must be released with the hand below hip height and *no* extra pace generated through wrist action.

Striking

The regulation bat must be *dropped* in the marked square or a hoop before the running or walking begins. Pupils *must* be taught exactly what to do and the rule rigidly enforced. No one must throw the bat.

For simplicity only the batter should have a bat in hand, the next in order retrieving it for the next strike.

The rules allow for the next in order to have a bat. If this is done, the waiting batter must be 'isolated' from the rest of the team. A marked pitch should include an 'on-deck' circle for this purpose.

Running

Sliding towards the bases, as occurs in baseball, must not be allowed. Pupils should either stop with one foot in the square or hoop or, if intending to run on, place one foot in en route.

Fielding and catching

The softball, being quite large, is reasonably easy to hold in the hands and therefore to catch or to pick up. However, as the ball can be hit quite hard, minimum distances between fielders and batsmen of 10 metres are recommended. If the 'pitching' is restricted to simple lobbing, the catcher need not wear gloves but if the delivery is speeded up so that the trajectory is quite flat and hard, catching mittens should be worn. Catchers should only use the gloves in the correct way.

Equipment

Balls should be checked for tears, and taping on bats must not be worn or coming away. Gloves must fit properly and laces must always be intact and properly tied.

Stoolball

The *mini-stoolball* version of the game should be played. The boundaries, inter-wicket and bowling distances and, crucially, the height of the wickets (1.2 metres) are scaled down.

Stoolball bats and balls may be used but, for easier and safer development of the game, a tennis ball and, in the earlier stages, a playbat are recommended.

Equipment

Stoolball posts may be bought. If, however, they are made, great care must be exercised to ensure that

- the base is designed and constructed so that full stability is ensured; and
- the target plate is attached to the post in a totally secure manner.

Bowling

Bowling must take place at the regulation distance for pupils of this age, 6 metres, and never any closer.

Fielding

As with all striking games, it is recommended that pupils field a minimum distance from the bat, in this case 10 metres. When the hard stoolball is used, the backstop must wear gloves.

(Swedish) longball

This excellent fast moving and exciting game has an obvious in-built danger. As players can be eliminated through being *hit* by the ball, if full care is not exercised an injury may be sustained.

In the past the game has been played with a tennis ball, allowing fast hard throwing to hand and at the person. It is recommended that either

- if the ball is to be thrown at a person
  - it should be soft rubber
  - it should be lobbed underarm only (i.e. at the person)
  - the distance of throwing towards a person should be limited to a maximum of 5 metres
  - the target area should be the legs
  or
- alternative methods of getting players out should be used e.g. before the hitter reaches the end line or returns to the base line
  - throwing and catching the ball a number of times possibly having to include fielders beyond each end line or on the corner markers
    or
  - achieving other forms of targets such as rolling or bouncing the ball between or into hoops, skittles etc. a number of times.

Section D: Net games

Games using a net (or a safe alternative) that might reasonably be expected to be played in primary schools include:

- battington
- badminton
- padder tennis
- short tennis.

The games and developmental skills practices may involve the use of playbats, special racquets or the hands and either balls of different sizes and types or shuttlecocks.

Playing areas

The games and practices would normally take place on the playground. Special care must be taken regarding the siting and form of the practices or games to ensure that balls and shuttles do not constitute a danger to other groups operating at the same time.

If any form of tennis or badminton is played in a school hall as a club activity, close attention must be paid to any projecting fixtures or equipment round the edges. It may be necessary to move the equipment and put padding round extending buttresses.

As with all games the playing areas and immediate surrounds should be free from all hazards (such as shuttles that are not being used).

Equipment

Posts and nets

All the posts to which the nets are attached must be totally stable and, where necessary, should be set up facing in the correct direction (e.g. badminton posts with the long base section facing inwards). The correct posts and net for some activities such as short tennis and badminton can be purchased, either as part of a set or separately. These can also be used for games like battington and padder tennis and other activities requiring moderately high and low nets.

NB Without a properly stabilised base, collision with a net may pull posts over in an inward direction. For this reason, posts manufactured for other purposes, such as netball, should NEVER be used.

All nets must be free from holes, tight and properly secured to the posts.

Safe alternatives to nets

It is possible to use alternatives to nets which can allow a whole class to work safely on practices or simple games. These include:

- *Ropes:* The simplest way of creating a clearance target is to place a rope on the ground, either on a painted line or on its own, possibly as the centre line of a court with a marked perimeter (usually a rectangle divided into two halves or quarters). This is a totally safe way of developing cooperation activities as well as simple and made-up games.

- *Benches:* One or two benches, end to end, can be used to give a low and stable clearance target. NB Benches must *never* be placed on top of each other to create a higher net equivalent.
- *Canes with cones or skittles:* Canes, taped at the ends, or laths can be placed on the cones or at different heights in the grooves in the skittles. The latter may be secured with tape.

Condition of equipment

All racquets, bats, balls and shuttles must be in good condition.

Specific activities

In order to both allow the children better opportunities to develop skills and motivation and to reduce the chances of balls or shuttles creating danger, the following safe practices are recommended.

Playbat practices and games

Many different balls, ranging from tennis through rubber to plastic may be used with wooden or plastic play or flat bats. The type of ball used would reflect the stage of learning and age of the pupil and, particularly, the nature of the activity.

Where partners or a foursome are aiming to score as many 'hits' in a row as possible by volleying or allowing one bounce – over lines, ropes, single benches or a low net i.e. *cooperating* – all types of balls may be used.

If the pupils are *competing*, tennis and rubber balls must only be used in a very restricted and clearly marked court area and all 'shots' must be played underarm following a bounce of the ball (i.e. no volleying). Tennis balls that are hit hard with a drive or smash action can travel very quickly and can be dangerous both to other players in the group who are in close proximity and to fellow classmates working independently.

To play a 'proper' game with playbats, similar in nature to padder tennis and allowing a full range of strokes, plastic airflow ('gamester') or foam balls should be used.

Short tennis

Only when sufficient space is available for the recommended court dimensions should short tennis be played. The special plastic racquets and foam balls should always be used.

Battington

Battington, a derivative of badminton using shuttles but playbats instead of racquets, can be safely developed in a similar way to ball skills: hitting in pairs and fours over a rope, followed successively by a low net and finally a net set at the same height as for badminton. Posts and nets must be of the type designed for badminton. As has been made clear above, improvising with different types of posts and/or ropes instead of nets can be very dangerous.

Short badminton

The 'short' or a suitably modified version of badminton should be played. Light racquets and slow flight shuttles are recommended.

Games involving large balls

Where games are played involving the throwing of large balls over the high net with the aim of avoiding the opponents on the other side and hitting the floor, the throwing action should be underarm.

Direction and spacing of games

Net games should be played in parallel, lengthways, with adequate space between each unit, never end to end. Alternatively, they may be played as part of a varied group work set-up as shown in Appendix C.

¤ Summary of major points for all types of games

1   *Surfaces and pitch conditions* should be both safe and suited to the activity.
2   *Adequate space* must be allowed between activities and between activities and surrounds.
3   If groups of pupils are having to work in close proximity to other groups, roads or residential or school buildings, *special restrictions* in regard to aspects such as direction of play and type of ball *may have to be applied*.
4   Equipment should only be used for the *purposes for which it was designed*.
5   Activities and areas should be matched to *pupils' abilities and needs*.
6   Special provisions (e.g. conditioning of a game) may have to be made in order to cater for *SEN (including disabled) pupils*.
7   It is recommended that *tackling should not be taught* in soccer or rugby and that, in the case of the latter, only non-tackling small-sided games are played. NB Special attention must be given to conditioning activities if tackling is taught.
8   *Teachers must not take an active competitive role* in games or practices, only joining in briefly when it is necessary to demonstrate a pass or a movement.
9   Very great care must be taken over the *securing and maintenance of equipment*, particularly posts and goals.
10 *Ropes should not be tied across* posts to improvise goals or nets.
11 When appropriate, *use soft rubber or tennis balls to develop skills* and, wherever possible, when playing games.
12 *Protective gear must be worn when necessary* and, specifically, when hard balls are used in striking games.
13 *Checks on readiness for play* should be made.
14 *Pupils waiting turns* in striking games must be 'contained' in a safe area.
15 *Minimum distances* between batters and fielders must be maintained.

9   Chasing activities and relays

Activities of this type are very much enjoyed by pupils. Providing the necessary basic and activity-specific precautions are taken, there is no reason why these activities should not be totally safe.

Demonstrations should be used to show the children exactly what to do. At times, it may be appropriate for the pupils to go through a procedure at walking pace or at a slow jog before competing against other teams.

¤ Golden rules for chasing games and relays

These rules apply to all activities of this type.

1   *No movements* (running, jumping etc.) should ever be made *in a backward direction.*
2   *Pupils must not carry other pupils* when moving about. A piggyback position may be taken up in static positions providing the pupils are capable of taking the weight and have practised doing so in non-competitive situations. (NB It must be ensured that the smallest pupil in a class is not put in a position in which she or he may attempt to take the weight of the heaviest.)
3   There should be *no running or other forms of movement to make deliberate contact with walls* or other fixed objects.
4   *Pupils should not form extended lines through holding hands.* Pupils on the end of such lines may be pulled round at speed and lose balance or collide with other team members. A maximum of three should be allowed to operate in this way.
5   *No activities that involve the ability to balance* (e.g. moving along a bench rib) *should be attempted in a competitive situation.* This is extremely dangerous!
6   *Pupils must never be asked to move on to and off or directly over three-dimensional objects,* such as benches or boxes, as part of an obstacle race, either against the clock or each other. Serious injuries are known to have occurred from this practice.
7   *Pupils must not be asked to carry heavy objects* such as mats or benches as part of a competitive activity.
8   *Pupils should not be tied together* at any points of the body. It is acceptable to attempt to keep a piece of small apparatus wedged between parts of the body (e.g. shoulder or hips) when moving from A to B.
9   *Surfaces should be suitable.* For example, concrete would not be suitable for this type of activity.
10   *If certain skills are required for the activity* (e.g. dribbling or passing) *they should be within the compass of all the participants* and should have been mastered in a non-competitive environment first.
11   *'Pirates',* involving pupils chasing other class members on gymnastic apparatus, *is unacceptably hazardous and should never be sanctioned.*

Chasing games

Space

There should be adequate space available to ensure that collisions do not occur in any given activity.

For example, when a number of large hoops (say, one per child) are placed on the ground and pupils asked to move in and out or between them, there should be at least 2 metres between adjacent hoops.

Outer perimeter

The outer perimeter of the action area should be at least 2 metres away from any walls or other fixed objects. This should be defined by painted lines and/or markers.

Tag games

Contact

When being chased, for example in an activity where the object is to grasp braids tucked into the waistbands of pairs of shorts or to touch the torso, pupils must not be allowed to use the arms to fend off or grapple with a chaser. This not only defeats the object of the game but is dangerous.

Collecting braids is recommended for this type of game. It allows for continuous activity, with pupils who have been caught getting back in the game, and also avoids virtually all possibility of pushing. It is also recommended that the chasers wear bibs or braids for identification.

Dodgeball activities

These range from full class versions, through groups of, say, 5 or 6, to *He*, a pairs activity. As in all games activities, groups and pairs must be matched for ability.

Equipment

Only large soft balls must be used in the class and group games, and a small soft ball or a beanbag in a game such as *He* where one child pursues another until a 'hit' is made and the positions are reversed.

Method and organisation

- All throwing at the target must be done underhand.
- The target may be restricted to below the knees, legs only or below the waist depending on the activity.
- When playing the whole class versions, those starting as chasers and those who have been hit wear bibs or braids. The game stops when there are still 5 or 6 uncaught. This avoids too much crowding and creates more winners.
- When playing in intermingling groups (i.e. 4 or 5 passing and running, aiming to hit one 'target' child) each group has different coloured bibs or braids in order to distinguish and avoid others.

- Beanbags are excellent as children learn *He*, as they do not roll away.

Relays

There are many different types of relay, utilising

- different numbers of participants;
- different modes of operation (e.g. pupils moving just once in each competition or continuously up to a maximum of four turns or remaining in position);
- different formats (e.g. with teams lining up in parallel or in the form of a geometrical shape, such as a circle, square or hexagon, or in and out of an agility circuit).

There are many pitfalls to avoid and accidents have occurred because the correct procedures have not been followed. By always following certain basic rules, however, relays can be organised safely.

Organisation

The aim should be to keep teams as small as possible:

- when operating one at a time, once only or continuously, teams should consist of no more than three. This allows each child more turns as well as being safer. (NB Working in pairs is ideal in many straight forward out and back relays.)
- where objects are passed down the line or all work together in unison, teams should consist of up to four pupils.

In parallel

A very safe and simple way to start relays and establish conforming to the correct procedure is to pass objects down lines of three, or more usually four, pupils who stay in the same place.

- Beanbags, which do not roll away when dropped, may be passed through the legs, overhead or from side to side or slid along the floor.
- Development may involve passing or rolling balls of different sizes, passing or sliding quoits, with the pupils standing or sitting on the floor or, possibly, a bench.
- The next stage would be for the back member to run to the front with the process repeated until the original formation is achieved, thus introducing simple controlled movement.

Further development

Moving away from, and back to, the partner or team

When working singly in this way, pupils should ideally run round or touch with the hand an obstacle (skittle, cone, marker dome or beanbag). Alternatively, if lines exist at the correct distances they may be touched by the hand or foot/feet.

To cut out any unfair advantage gained by team members moving out to meet the incoming runner, and to make the activity much safer, pupils should always run *past*

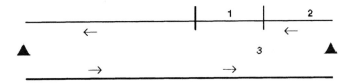

Figure 9.1 Short course full circuit relay format

the next in line, move round another obstacle or touch a line behind, and then return to touch the next in line or, better, pass on an object such as a quoit or beanbag (see Figure 9.1). Passing should always be left to right or right to left in order to avoid running up directly behind the competitor.

The continuous version, with a minimum of three members, shown in Figure 9.2, works on the same principle with handovers occurring at both ends.

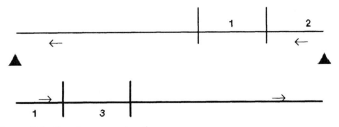

Figure 9.2 Continuous relay format

When a ball is being dribbled in some way (using feet or a stick, by bouncing etc.), a system must be devised which prevents the ball being hit or thrown to the next competitor while still some distance away. Moving round the back marker helps considerably. Placing the ball dead in a hoop on the floor or having to push it through two close markers, depending on the nature of the activity, is better still.

Positioning

As much distance as is practicable should be left between teams: 2 metres minimum is recommended for all the activities, with 3 metres or more being desirable for those involving ball control.

Sufficient distance must be left between the finishing line and any hazard, such as a wall, in order to pull up safely before contact is made (see chapter 10, *Track events*, *Track lay-out*). When short of space, safety can be ensured by placing the finishing line at the mid-point between the two cones.

Geometric shapes

There are different ways of using such a set-up.

Figure 9.3 shows how two teams can safely use a simple square. Teams of four are shown but threes could be equally effective and allow more turns per person. Team A, B, C, D in the centre pass the ball as many times as possible while Team 1, 2, 3, 4 run round the cones forming the square, one at a time. The first team member, 1, is shown running round the square; 2 is in position to receive the baton, quoit or ball when 1

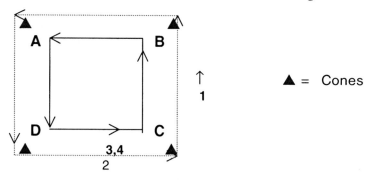

Figure 9.3 Passing versus running relay format

completes the lap, 3 and 4 are waiting for their turns, positioned safely inside the 'running' line drawn between the corner markers. When 2 passes the first cone, 3 moves out and takes up the position for receiving the baton and 1 takes up a safe position inside the 'line'.

Circuits

Negotiating agility (running) or skills circuits as part of a relay is normally quite safe – providing that sufficient distance is left between each set of markers (2–3 metres) and the pupils have mastered the skills involved (rolling, steering or bouncing a large ball, or dribbling a ball with feet or stick).

An easy and safe way to set up markers is to use the lines on a grid (see chapter 8, *Invasion games* and Appendix B, *Playground markings*).

10 Athletics

This chapter is divided into sections as follows:

A   General principles
B   Track events
C   Jumping events
D   Throwing events
E   Potted sports

Section A: General principles

> A young child's first experience of athletics should be an
> integrated play element incorporating the basic material
> of athletics and the action possibilities of the child within
> a wider movement experience
>
> (Key Stage 2, *ESAA Handbook* 2001)

As the *ESAA Handbook* makes clear, the stress should be on experiencing a wide range of ways of jumping, throwing and moving over the ground. This will be achieved through direction and/or limitation of the parameters of tasks and experimentation (the NC states that pupils must be given opportunities to invent new ways of jumping, throwing etc.). The initial emphasis should be on attempting simple modes with a gradual move to more experimentation and the learning of simple specific skills (e.g. scissors high jump) and control. It is possible to attempt certain established events but, more often, this will be done in a modified form that enables the pupils to both work productively and safely in regard to physical limitations and actual practice conditions.

There should not be a strong influence on individual competition, but rather on self-improvement against known yardsticks. This is both educationally sound and safer.

- Pupils designing their own activities should be aware of limits that are imposed in respect of safety.
- Most events would be done on a field or a suitable synthetic surface that may be part of or adjacent to a school playground, or a proper athletics track. A number of events that can be suitably done in sports halls and, in some cases, on playgrounds are also included.
- As in all aspects of PE, it is essential that activities take place far enough away from walls and other items of equipment to ensure there is no danger of contact.

Supervision

Teachers should ensure that, when run in parallel, the number of events is limited to what can be effectively managed, particularly when throwing is involved.

The pupils should be within easy communication distance from the teacher.

Sports day

Exactly the same conditions apply as in lessons.

It is essential that barriers are erected to stop spectators from encroaching on competition areas and that ALL are made aware of their purpose.

The most important staff function is to ensure that any child who is not participating at a given time is being supervised.

Section B: Track events

These include individual, relay and hurdles races. The relays are particularly valuable as, through sensible team selection, they give everyone an opportunity of gaining success.

Surfaces

Working surfaces must be even and smooth, free from holes or debris and afford a reasonable grip.

Track lay-out

Short races of 20–80 metres can be done in a straight line. Any races above that distance should normally be round a track.

Using *lanes* is strongly recommended for races that are run in a straight line or up to once round the track – avoiding the possibility of collisions. (NB In the absence of a circular track it is possible to run up and down a straight track, rounding a marker at the ends.) Only one child should be allowed to run in a lane and/or run round a marker at one time, and pupils should be clearly instructed in the need to remain in their own lanes.

In the absence of lanes, a temporary circuit may be marked out using cones. When groups of children are running together, however, there must be no sharp angles, only gentle bends following a set radius connected by perfectly straight lines.

Finishing lines in any kind of race should be clearly indicated. They should be a sufficient distance from any wall or fixed object to allow the children to pull-up with plenty of room to spare. This will vary with age.

Race organisation

Starting

Starting guns can cause injuries and should not be used. A clapperboard can easily be made (two pieces of solid wood hinged together with handles on the outside surfaces) to simulate a gun, or the time-honoured 'On Your Marks', 'Set', 'Go!' used.

Finishing

When a finishing tape is required, thin *wool* that breaks on contact should be used. Synthetic yarn, string, ribbon and other unbreakable materials must *never* be substituted. Care should be taken to ensure that the wool is at chest height or below, not where contact may be with the neck or face.

Distance

Pupils in this age span should not engage in fast running over distances beyond 100 metres (see *Relays, Continuous relays* below and Appendix A). It is safe to run longer distances of up to a mile, depending on ability, but this should be at a slow, even rate (jogging pace) and under the direct control of a teacher.

Hurdles

The rudiments of hurdling can be successfully taught to most top KS2 pupils. A fair proportion can develop the ability to hurdle well.

Hurdling can be developed very safely, providing the correct approach is adopted and equipment used in the right way. Accidents have occurred because of failure to do either or both of these.

Hurdling development

The method outlined below has been used successfully for many years and is recommended by national coaches. It allows for a lot of flexibility, particularly in regard to height and easy opportunity to run over the barriers at very low levels. Development is in five main stages.

First stage: Three sets of three skipping ropes are laid on the ground, with 3 metres between each set of ropes. The distance between the ropes in each set will vary to cater for the ability range in a class (see Figure 10.1).

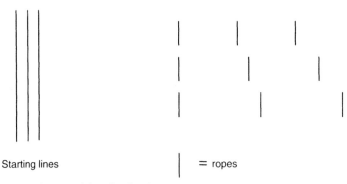

Starting lines　　　　　　　　　| = ropes

Figure 10.1 Staggered interval hurdle development

Pupils run, quite fast, over the ropes, changing lines if necessary, until they establish the correct distance for a four stride pattern – one over the rope, three between. Inter-rope distance adjustments may be made. This can be most easily and safely done using a hurdles grid as shown in Figure 10.2, with the distance between the ropes (and, later, foam barriers and hurdles) gradually widening. Pupils know exactly where to position the rope for each attempt.

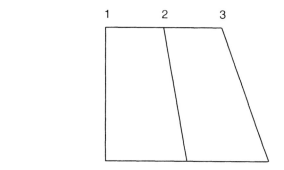

Figure 10.2 A hurdles grid

Second stage: It is now necessary to introduce a low-level barrier for the pupils to *run* over (hurdling is sprinting, not jumping).

This can be done by using triangular foam 'hurdles' of the type used for sports hall competitions or, better, initially, as they allow easy flexibility and can be used at low heights, squared foam strips suspended across pegs attached to poles or skittles or a combination of the two. (NB Canes or laths placed on cones or pegs or on the grooves of wire skittles or any other solid barrier should *never* be used. There is a high risk of the object being caught up between the thighs and causing the child to fall. Nor should a cane or other solid barrier be tied to any kind of support – this is highly dangerous.)

The pupils start, ideally, at a very low height, say around 10 cm, running over the middle point and changing groups if necessary, establishing which leg should lead. It is important that this is established at this early stage before higher barriers and proper hurdles are attempted.

Third stage: Three parallel starting lines, 1 metre apart, are introduced and pupils encouraged to find the one that suits them in regard to running smoothly over the foam strips (see Figures 10.1 and 10.2).

Fourth stage: The barrier height is gradually raised by about 10 cm at a time, to a maximum of 40–45 cm. The hurdling technique is developed in stages as the height is raised through the gradual introduction of the correct leg, arm and body actions.

Fifth stage: The children then move on to using lightweight or foam hurdles set at low heights appropriate to KS2.

NB Hurdles must not be weighted to prevent them blowing over. Practice should only take place on a virtually wind-free day.

Golden rules for hurdling

- Pupils must develop the correct run-up and stride pattern between barriers and a reasonable technique before attempting real hurdles. Not all pupils will be able to do this.
- Pupils must never attempt to clear a hurdle back to front.
- Never use unsuitable equipment (e.g. canes on pegs or tied to skittles or posts, hockey sticks on cones, damaged hurdles).
- Only ever practise on completely dry surfaces. Never practise on tarmac or concrete.
- Never allow a child to 'just have a go' with actual hurdles.
- Ensure that one set of children have completed their attempts before the next set start.
- Only a teacher who has covered hurdles development as part of a recognised course should teach the event.

Relays

There are two types of relay which are suitable for older primary school pupils, *shuttle* – modified to ensure that the activity is totally safe and the possibility of cheating is eliminated – and standard *round the track*. The latter can also be developed into a continuous form with each pupil running 3–4 times before the relay is completed as opposed to the normal once. Junior batons, quoits or even beanbags, if placed in the hand and not thrown, can be safely used as the object to be passed from hand to hand.

In both cases, it is essential that the object used should be transferred to the opposite hand (left–right, right–left) with the incoming runner to the side of the outgoing runner and *not* directly behind, where collisions or tripping can occur.

Modified shuttles

These are organised in the same way as the continuous relay described and illustrated in chapter 9. In this case, the distance is increased to 60–80 metres (i.e. 30–40 metres between the end markers) and teams of 3 or 4 compete. Shuttles can be run either with two pupils starting at each end (each runner completes half circuits, with a stress on baton changing) or with three at one end (each runner completes full circuits).

As the baton is passed on to the outgoing runner from behind and not, as in the case of standard shuttles, face to face, the possibility of colliding is completely eliminated. As there is no longer anything to be gained from leaving early to meet the incoming runner, the endemic cheating experienced when doing basic shuttles no longer occurs.

*   In order not to impede the runner while waiting their turns, pupils sit or stand in direct line with the markers as shown in Figures 10.3. and 10.4.
*   The pupil who is to receive next moves out of the waiting line and into the pathway of running indicated in Figure 10.3. Doing this ensures that the team members who are not involved in the changeover do not impede the transfer of the baton or the running in any way.
*   In Figure 10.3 the system used when each runner completes a full circuit is shown. The first runner no. 1, having started from line b1, is shown having almost completed a full circuit and about to hand over to outgoing runner no. 2. No. 2 has moved from the waiting position between the markers to a position in the changeover box in order to receive the baton. The third team member no. 3 remains seated or standing between the markers and will move into the box only when no. 2 is approaching the second marker in the circuit. No. 1, meanwhile, after handing over the baton, moves in line between the markers.
*   The system shown in Figure 10.4 where the runners are only doing half circuits is based on the same principle. No. 1 will hand over to no. 2 and sit down behind no. 4. No. 2 will move round and hand over to no. 3 in the second box and then remain there waiting for the next runner. No. 3 hands over to no. 4 who has moved into the first box and the process is repeated with each runner having at least two turns.
*   It is recommended that the changeover box distance should be from 10–12 metres in length and that the second line (e.g. b2 Figure 10.3) the finishing point of the race.
*   Marked lines, cones (placed in line with the markers), or, even, beanbags are safe ways of marking the changeover box limits in this type of relay.

This is a very safe way of teaching the principles and guarantees many opportunities to both run and practise passing a baton or substitute object from hand to hand.

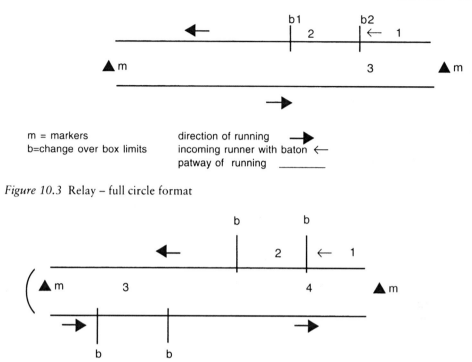

Figure 10.3 Relay – full circle format

Figure 10.4 Relay – continuous format

Low foam hurdles, using one or two in one or both directions, can also be incorporated into the modified shuttle format.

Standard relays

Standard relays involve running round the track using marked lanes and changeover 'boxes'. Such boxes must be marked with white lines, braids or beanbags but not, in this case, cones or skittles which may cause an obstruction.

Providing the pupils stay in their designated lanes, change to alternate hands and, initially, only run one lap, there should be no problems in organising this type of relay.

Continuous relays

The ideal way for KS2 pupils to experience 'distance' running is to do it as a team event – an ongoing relay. Teams of four or five (one more than the number of stations) keep running until all have had a designated number of turns. Each pupil rests for three or four times as long as the running phase.

Improvised track events

Pupils may be encouraged to 'invent' track events. It is *essential*, however, that on no account should there be any running backwards or over obstacles, continuous jumping or hopping, or carrying other pupils or heavy objects.

Fun events (such as three-legged and sack races or races which involve balancing objects while running) that in the past often featured in sports days, tend to have a fairly high risk level and should be avoided.

Various ways of skipping may be developed safely.

Section C: Jumping events

Pupils of this age can safely and usefully practise a whole range of jumps, including standing and one step types as well as those that utilise a run-up.

Because of the pressure brought to bear on the foot and ankle, it is recommended that pupils of this age *do not attempt the running triple jump*.

Regardless of the form of jump, only a limited number of attempts should be made. This is particularly so if the jump is multi-phase (e.g. standing triple jump, three double foot jumps).

Taking off

Provided surfaces are flat and dry and offer a good grip, take-offs for many horizontal jumps that involve standing or one step take-offs may be made from playground surfaces and hall floors, as well as grass and the rubber composition surfaces found on purpose built jumping areas.

Horizontal jumps

Ideally, long and other forms of horizontal jumping should be done using a short run take-off, from the side of a long pit filled with sand of a suitable type (see *Landings* below). This allows a number of children to jump at the same time. The take-off surface should be suitable and the pit of sufficient width to ensure there is room to land and move forward safely. The 'outside edge' of the pit should be protected (see below). Few schools have access to such wide pits, however, and running and jumping from the side into a standard pit would be highly dangerous. Only jumping from the ends into such pits, one at a time, should be permitted.

Take-off boards

If a take-off board is used in long jumping, it must be securely embedded, in good condition (i.e. not splintering), flush with the run-up and painted in a colour that can be easily seen.

If the area immediately adjacent to the board has been worn away, leaving an exposed ridge, the board must not be used until the necessary re-packing, flattening and rolling is carried out.

All boards and take-off points must be within easy reach of the pit for ALL the pupils involved.

Run-ups

Run-ups should be flat, smooth and in good repair, with no loose grit or holes. If the run-up is grass, it must be cut short and always be dry enough to provide a firm grip.

Run-ups should not be made on hard surfaces (e.g. concrete). Take-offs for horizontal or high jumps should not be made from bare earth where grass has been worn away.

High Jumps

Only high jump styles that feature landing on the feet must be used in sand. *Scissors* (with a full run-up or shortened run-up of 1–3 strides) is recommended.

Other safe 'styles' using taking off from one or two feet and landing on one or two feet can be developed via suggestion.

Most jumping would be done at fairly low heights with some opportunity at the top of KS2 for certain pupils to measure their ability against higher challenges.

On no account must styles which involve landing on the body or improvised diving, such as the Fosbury Flop, be attempted, regardless of bar height or approach distance.

Care should be taken that only one pupil at a time attempts to clear the bar. As pupils may approach from left or right or even the centre, a routine must be established (possibly all pupils together in the centre before the next to practise or compete takes up a starting position).

Landings

Sand

Sand is an ideal medium for high jump and horizontal jumps at this age level. However, it must always be

- contained in a pit;
- a *sharp* type of sand, i.e. non-caking;
- regularly dug over so that it is yielding.

It may be necessary to clean and disinfect and, also, top up the sand periodically. When pits are in use, great care must be taken over operating conditions.

- Checks for 'foreign objects' must be made before all periods of use.
- To ensure jumping ceases while raking is done, a cone should be placed on the run-up or in front of the high jump bar.
- Run-ups should be completely free of grit, water and objects (e.g. tape measures, brushes or markers).
- It should be ensured that digging and raking implements are placed at least three metres from the landing area, with teeth or tines down.
- If the pit has hard edges (e.g. wood) these must be flush with the ground and covered by a sufficient thickness of appropriate protective material (e.g. foam rubber chips in sacks).

Beds and mats

Landing beds, specifically designed for high jump, *are not recommended* for primary school high jumping.

It is recommended that crash mats should *never* be used for any type of jump landing. There is a danger of turning or breaking the ankle.

Indoors, or on playgrounds or fields or all-weather surfaces without pits, a 2″ (5 cm) thick gymnastic mat may be used for standing or one step high jump – always landing on the feet. As into sand, the jumps can vary in form and feature one and two foot take-offs at different heights.

A 2″ (5 cm) or 1″ (2.5 cm) thick gymnastic mat may be used for broad jump or a short combination of movements from standing, finishing on two feet. All such mats must be in a good state of repair and must not slip on impact.

Equipment for jumping

High jump bars

The following may be used:

- *Round high jump bars*. Triangular high jump bars should not be used. Such bars must be in good condition.
- *Flexi-bars* are excellent for practice, providing the posts are properly secured and will not collapse inwards when contact is made with the bar.
- *Laths or canes* can be used on playgrounds or indoors. These should be protected at the ends, and placed on pegs attached to skittles or used with high jump posts.

Long jump aids

Bars or canes must never be placed or held across the run-up in order to encourage height. Large, very soft balls can be suspended from a pole and pupils encouraged to make contact with the chest.

Designing jumps

The national curriculum orders state that pupils should have opportunity to design their own jumps. If they wish to add numbers of double foot jumps, steps and hops together, run-ups should not be allowed.

Section D: Throwing events

The following pieces of equipment may be used in a variety of ways to create interesting modes of throwing and, possibly, competitions:

- balls of different weights, sizes and consistency;
- quoits;
- beanbags;
- soft 'Olympic' type implements manufactured for indoor use by primary age children, such as 200g shot (and 270g shot for Year 6 only) or 50g javelin;
- 2 metre 250g caber.

Normal metal 'Olympic' type throwing equipment (discus, hammer, javelin or shot) must *never* be used in primary schools.

Throwing for distance

Throwing with a short run-up

Pupils should start with tennis balls, and then possibly move through the heavier medium-hard rubber balls, to rounders, stoolball and cricket balls.

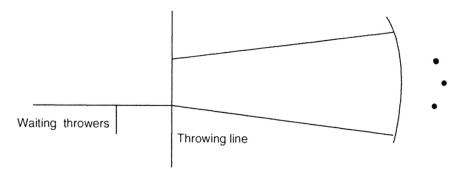

• = collectors

Figure 10.5 A lay-out for throwing – running or standing

- Ensure that pupils using hard balls have demonstrated an ability to throw straight.
- Ensure that collectors stand outside a prescribed 20–30 degree arc, or beyond a marked line a clear distance past the maximum distance expected.
- No thrower can move over the throwing line until all those designated to throw have done so (see figure 10.5).

Throwing from standing

All the activities suggested for throwing with a short run-up may also be done from standing with the same safety guidelines applying.

Additionally, there are many that can only be safely done from stationary positions. These include excellent ways of bringing in the hips and upper body, as well as the arms. For example:

- a soccer type throw-in;
- a two-handed throw, backwards over the head, using a size four football, netball or large soft ball;
- a two-handed throw from the side (like the last phase of the hammer) using only a large, soft ball.

NB For throws with a short run-up and from standing, there should be:

- *no* throwing from wet surfaces;
- *no returning* objects by throwing back to the designated throwing area.

Throwing from sitting

A large ball may be thrown from two hands forward or backwards or putted from the chest.

For indoors or playground, sit on a gymnastic mat. If the throw is backwards, allow room for the body to pivot and the shoulders to make contact with the mat.

Forward throws or puts can be made from sitting positions on a bench.

Throwing from kneeling

Many types of throw, including those where the object is moved round the side of the body before release (e.g. one-handed – using a discus type action, or – two-handed – using a hammer type action with, say, a ball in a net), as opposed to directly forwards, can be done from a kneeling position.

Throwing for accuracy

A safe way of developing skill or competing, particularly where space is limited, is to stress accuracy rather than distance. Different balls can be used, aiming for parallel lines, hoops, bins, marked concentric circles on the ground or walls etc. Beanbags, staying where they land, are very useful.

Designing throws

The national curriculum states that pupils should have the opportunity to design their own ways of throwing different objects. This can be safely done with soft balls of different sizes, quoits, beanbags and the soft 'Olympic' implements, plus shuttlecocks and airflows in restricted areas – aiming for accuracy as well as distance.

Particular care must be exercised when a slinging type action is used (say with a quoit imitating part of a discus action). No pupils should be within throwing distance of the performer in the sector to the side of the action of the throw.

Section E: Potted sports

Potted sports is based on teams of three or four, matched in ability, competing in a variety of events, usually selected so that a minimum of space is required. It is possible for each team member to score a different number of points in each event according to the standard achieved (each being based on time, or distance, or height). Traditionally, potted sports have been based on athletic events, many modified (such as one foot take off jumps and throwing from sitting) but it is quite possible to include ball skills such as dribbling.

The key is to ensure that sufficient space is left between each event to ensure that one does not impinge on another (e.g. a two-handed throw from sitting is normally quite straight but will need a reasonable margin of error).

There must be sufficient space to return to a waiting area without crossing the path of other competitors.

The events are set up in the same way as for the group work outlined in Appendix C.

Important considerations for potted sports

- All pupils should have practised all the events before competing and fully understand the procedures. The pupils should be able to demonstrate proficiency at any skills being tested.
- Only one pupil in each group should compete at one time.
- Pupils should always move in the prescribed direction.
- No dynamic balance activities based on time (e.g. running or hopping along a balance beam or bench rib) should be performed.

11 Outdoor and adventurous activities

Jes Woodhouse

Why outdoor and adventurous activities?

Activities based upon adventure, exploration and challenge offer a learning environment centred on the very things many children seek naturally. A structured programme of adventure activities can help children satisfy their desire to meet challenging situations whilst also learning to keep themselves and others safe. There are many low-risk adaptations of adventurous activities available. These activities can provide a sense of adventure and challenge for pupils, and perhaps a subjective sense of danger, but, at the same time, may be low in risk and infinitely suitable for use within and around the immediate environment of the school by teachers who are not experienced in outdoor activities.

The aim of this chapter is to show the major safety considerations related to the provision of these kinds of adventure activities.

Appropriate adventure activities for use at key stages one and two

Given appropriate conditions and under the guidance of teachers with activity expertise, children's horizons are boundless. It may be claimed that *any* adventure activity *can* be appropriate for children – but this must be qualified with regard to the context in which you will be working. An 'appropriate' activity should be seen as one that matches well the resources of all concerned, i.e. the learner's and the teacher's, as well as equipment and environmental resources.

In the school setting at key stages one and two, children will probably best be helped to develop skills and qualities by building camps, looking for hidden treasure, helping each other escape from dragons or crossing rivers of poisonous custard as well as taking the time to marvel at some of the beauties nature provides.

Within this chapter, reference to some adventure activities as illustrative examples should provide a hint of what is available, but, for a truly comprehensive guide to the range of activities on offer, you should refer to some of the resources listed in Appendix F. Always work to your own capabilities and if you do possess a degree of expertise in a specific adventurous activity, there is nothing to prevent you utilising this to assist pupils' learning. Just make sure you follow the safety procedures laid down by the recognised governing body and/or your local governing education authority.

A framework for planning challenging and safe adventure activities

Pupils' needs and capabilities

The first thing to consider when planning adventure activities in schools is the children. This may appear obvious but there can be a tendency to think first that 'the blindfold trust walk is a good activity, I'll do that with the pupils next week'. Assess pupils' learning needs, their capabilities, stages of development and the like before then deciding that a blindfold trust walk would be just the thing to help them develop. Try hard to establish this as a vital first stage of the planning process. It will also be necessary at this stage to consider the implications of any existing medical conditions.

Teacher's knowledge and capabilities

Consider your own knowledge and capabilities. If adventure activities are new to you, select those with which you feel comfortable and able to assess any potential risk. It should be the children's imagination running wild, not your own anxieties. Seek advice from other members of staff who may have some experience. Alternatively, consult with local advisory staff or staff from a recognised local adventure activities centre. As your experience of adventure activities grows, so will your confidence and your ability to set more complex challenges but, to begin with, select tasks that are easy to administer, observe and control.

Adventure activities

Select activities that are related clearly to the proposed learning focus. Many adventure activities can be adapted to suit the capabilities of pupils (and the teacher), whatever their age and, as a result, pupils might encounter the same activity across the key stages. For example, a 'spider's web' could be a great way for younger children to develop a sense of controlled movement as they endeavour to crawl through the lower sections without getting 'stuck' to the strands. As the children develop strength and responsibility they could encounter what is fundamentally the same activity but on this occasion they could be lifting, supporting and lowering each other to enable safe passage through some of the higher gaps in the web. Of course, any activity that requires pupils to bear weight, whether it be the weight of themselves, their peers or items of equipment, will require you to first make a judgement as to whether or not they are physically, socially and emotionally prepared for such a task.

Environment and supporting resources

Adventure activities generally benefit from the use of supporting resources. Indeed, if you are fortunate enough to have fixed gymnastic apparatus or items of gymnastic equipment, you have a fantastic opportunity to create adventurous environments within the confines of the school building. However, it is important to remember that any piece of equipment must always be utilised for the purpose for which it was originally designed.

Apparatus and equipment must be sited with due regard for pupils' movement onto, across, through and off a particular piece and no activities should be planned that would involve children in chasing, racing or rushing to beat time limits when working off the floor.

Patches of grass, small copses of trees, or *'natural' resources* within the school grounds, such as walls, may be used to support adventure activities. The same principles apply to these as to pupils' movement but there will be the need for even greater consideration, as the fundamental purposes of many of these are not designed for such activities. If, however, they are not used to support children's weight but to provide a backdrop to the activities and an environment for the children to work within, there should be little risk. With thorough checking of any natural resources, however, it may be possible to bring aspects of the environment into the activities. In the same vein, items such as barrels, poles, milk crates and planks can be used in adventure activities.

If you elect to use either the natural environment or items of equipment such as these, it is of paramount importance that you set up and check any proposed arrangement, using appropriate amounts of weight if applicable. You may eventually begin to see the potential in the school site as an adventure playground. Indeed, it may be perfectly possible to utilise the school's natural resources to create challenging learning sites but such a venture would first require consultation with a local authority adviser or a playground professional.

Grassy areas and copses can be great places for building camps or conducting 'night lines', but it is important to check the area thoroughly, especially with regard to hidden rocks or other protrusions in the ground, or any stiff, sharp branches that may be projecting at the height of the children. Also, the slope of the ground and conditions underfoot will need to be considered in relation to any trust or support activities that might be planned. If you decide to use tent-pegs in the construction of shelters, the plastic variety should be employed with rubber, as opposed to metal, mallets.

Consider appropriate clothing for pupils, especially footwear. As with all physical activities, pupils need to wear clothing that allows them to move freely whilst affording suitable protection from the demands of the activity, other pupils or the environment.

It makes a great deal of sense to share decisions over safety with the pupils themselves. They can then begin to develop an increasing responsibility for this important aspect of their physical education.

Lesson structure

Ensure the lesson format does not place any pressure on you or the children to rush through the planned content. Conversely, the lesson structure should not be so loose that pupils drift aimlessly and begin to lose attention. You want them to develop an awareness of the dynamic nature of the adventure environment and to this end you should ensure a purposeful air throughout the lesson. You may feel the need for a tight structure if you are new to adventure activities, and this is perfectly understandable. However, you should still ensure that there is room within your structure for children to develop at a pace suited to them. Also remember, you will be trying to encourage the pupils to take a considered approach to the solving of adventure-related problems, some of which should involve reflection on risk and safety issues. The worst example to set would be that of rushing them through such important decisions.

Differentiation

Pupils differ in many ways and lesson content needs to take account of this. Aim to challenge pupils at levels appropriate to them – too low and they become bored, too high and they become fearful, both of which could have implications for safety. Set a generic learning focus for the whole group and then plan for subtle variations within the activities themselves to take account of differing stages of development between the pupils.

Decision-making

It may, however, be necessary to modify your approach. Decisions in the outdoors sometimes need to be made quickly – safety may demand it – and pupils need to progress towards making them – correctly – in a minimal amount of time. Once they approach this stage, you may well structure a lesson that deliberately puts pressure on the pupils with regard to the speed of their decision-making. The essential difference, however, is that you will be making an informed decision about the learning focus and the structure of the lesson. Any pressure on the pupils will have been considered carefully, a situation that is clearly different from that of placing undue pressure on pupils through ill-considered planning.

Pupil groupings

The inherently safe nature of school-based adventure activities means that they are suitable for class-sized groups, but the structure and management of these groups will require some thought. Pupils may be working in pairs or small groups, sometimes on the same activity and, at other times, on activities that may be structured slightly differently to take account of the pupil differences mentioned earlier. Give some thought to the pairings or groupings that will best work together. You are trying to create an exciting and challenging environment and this might arouse strong emotions in some.

Whilst you have to be careful about over-exciting pupils, you do want to engage their imagination and it is worth considering whether to group the more excitable pupils together, so you can keep a close eye on them, or whether it might be best to split them into groups with less excitable pupils.

There may be one 'higher risk' group or, to enable differing levels of challenge, you may set up one variation of an activity that is felt to be 'higher risk' than the rest. In either case, plan to site yourself nearer to that group or activity station to ensure close supervision, whilst still maintaining a position to observe, manage and feed back to the rest of the class. Time spent on helping children take increasing responsibility for their own and others' safety is always time well invested and will be particularly helpful to you in situations such as these.

Risk assessment

From a safety point of view, the *planning process* is an opportunity to think through carefully the implications of your learning focus, the capabilities of the children and yourself, the activities selected, resources and the working environment, the structure of the lesson and the ways in which pupils might be grouped. At each stage of the planning process, conduct a risk assessment and satisfy yourself that no obvious risk is present. Also think a little beyond the obvious to anticipate some of the more unpredictable things that pupils can do. As with any activity that might be new to you, it is advisable to take a dry run through the activity wherever possible as a means to developing a genuine feel for what might occur. If you suspect that risk could be present, you do not necessarily have to abandon any thought of using an activity. You can look for ways to control the risk and, in essence, adopt a 'risk management' strategy.

Adventure in action – the practicalities

Observation and vigilance

Dangers within adventure activities tend to arise when activities are presented to pupils with no prior reference to their capabilities and needs. By following the principles outlined in the previous section, you should be able to put together a lesson that will be wholly appropriate for your pupils and within which you should feel confident. Consequently, when the lesson takes place, your concern should be with two main watchwords – *observation* and *vigilance*. You will well know the nature of your class and should be in a good position to judge their mood as they embark on their adventures. Strike the right balance between firing up their imagination and not over-exciting them. Once happy the class is in the frame of mind to begin working responsibly, your planning should have left you feeling confident enough to set the ball rolling.

Equipment

Check any equipment to be used and also the working area to ensure there are no unwanted obstructions or intrusions. If equipment is set up as the lesson progresses, check it before the pupils begin work.

Teaching position

Teaching position is a paramount consideration within any physical education lesson and you should always have a sense of contact with each member of the class. A lesson that is heavily teacher-directed will probably see you in a position where the whole class is always immediately visible. This also applies when the pupils are working in groups at various stations. This is not difficult to achieve when working indoors, but is often more difficult when outdoors, especially if the pupils are engaged in a treasure hunt or orienteering-type activity. Obviously, you will take the children through a variety of progressions towards the time when you feel able to let them find their way around without close supervision. When this time comes, brief the children on the boundaries and safety rules to which they must adhere. Take up a fixed position that affords the widest view of the working environment and to which the children can return if a problem arises.

If you are working with younger children, extra adults may be available to assist. This can be of great help but helpers must always be briefed on the nature of the activities and any safety considerations. Satisfy yourself that they are suitably experienced to take on any role assigned and that they are of suitable character to be working with your pupils (see section on *Adult helpers* below).

Where there might be a variety of adventure activities going on in different locations outdoors, and where some of those activities might cause the pupils to be working out of sight, it is essential that those particular activities involve no predictable risk. Any activities that might involve pupils in supporting each other or working off the ground should be sited in such a way that you are in close contact with them, able to maintain a close eye and able to step in quickly or provide support should it be necessary. Throughout the lesson you should remain sensitive to the atmosphere and never hesitate to bring an activity to a halt if you feel that pupils are becoming overly competitive, oblivious to safety considerations or irresponsible in their approach.

Maintaining a sense of control

Remain vigilant with regard to the progress of the lesson in relation to your plan. Whilst you want to be in a position to respond flexibly wherever possible to the endeavours of the pupils, you don't want to let those endeavours create situations to which you may not have given prior consideration.

As always, the more experience you acquire, the more you will feel able to adopt a more flexible approach. If at any stage your observations and vigilance cause you to feel uneasy, bring things to a halt in a controlled manner and take time to consider your next move.

How was it? Where to next?

Observation, *assessment* and *evaluation* are not only essential to pupils' learning but, also, to processes that should enable you to ensure a safe working environment, as the nature of challenge becomes more complex. A well-structured, progressive programme should enable pupils to develop quite complex skills and a wide range of qualities within the school environment itself. This will depend on the expertise of the staff and the school environment, but there is no reason why primary-age pupils cannot ultimately be completing orienteering courses, practising their rope work skills or even camping overnight, all within the school grounds. Whilst this represents progression on one front, another logical step might be to move beyond the bounds of the school, both in terms of staffing and environment.

Adult helpers (AOTTs)

You might have access to nursery nurses, teaching assistants or parent helpers. Beyond this, you might bring expertise into the school in the form of a local climber, a member of staff from a local adventure centre or perhaps a representative from the British Orienteering Federation. Whatever the help, you must be satisfied that those assisting are suitable, that they will present no undue risk to your pupils, either in their methods of working or their character, and that they meet the requirements of the school and employer (normally a CRB enhanced disclosure certificate) (see chapter 1, *Adults other than teachers*).

If you decide to move beyond the bounds of the school, whether it be to a local park, a permanent orienteering course or to a recognised adventure activity centre, you will be best served if the venture is a clearly planned progression from the work carried out in school. As stated previously, you should have given thought initially to the needs of the pupils and, as a result, determined that their needs will be well met by a move into the wider environment.

Local environment

The same principles apply in terms of planning and supervision, but you will also need to consult local policies and procedures related to out-of-school activities, school visits and journeys. If you have a local Physical Education adviser or advisory teacher, they will be a useful reference point in this respect. A *preparatory visit* to the site or centre is essential if you are to assess fully the suitability of the venue and the level of any risk. Remember, pupils will need to be supervised closely throughout any such visit and if they are to be working in any way that spreads them out as a group, you will have to consider carefully the adult-pupil ratio. This shouldn't present a great problem if you are visiting a centre with its own specialist staff but a visit to a local park, for example, will almost certainly require you to seek the support of other adults so that pupils are not exposed to unnecessary risk. You might want to keep the supervision of older pupils 'at a distance', to enhance their sense of responsibility and independent action, but it is important for that supervision distance to remain within safe limits.

It might be that your chosen location is blessed with items of play or adventure equipment. Use of such equipment will require a thorough check of the equipment itself, along with any landing areas, which should be constructed of approved materials such as bark chippings or firm sponge. Remember, any equipment should be used for its intended purpose and you should consider carefully its appropriateness in helping pupils towards the achievement of particular learning goals.

Adventure activity centres

Adventure activity centres can provide opportunities for pupils to engage in more complex adventure games, recognised outdoor pursuits and, in some cases, residential experience. Centres can be found in both urban and rural environments.

As when venturing into the local environment, your first step should be to consult local policies and procedures as related to your proposed out-of-school activity, visit and/or journey. Talk with staff from the centre prior to your visit. A personal inspection is recommended strongly. It is best to approach the venture with a good idea of pupils' needs and the ways in which a centre visit might meet these. The centre should be prepared to accommodate those needs and be willing to structure a programme to suit your pupils. On a personal visit you can develop a feel for the centre as well as being able to check the following key factors:

* their health and safety policy and code of practice;
* public liability insurance;
* possession of a current licence from the *Adventure Activity Licensing Authority* (check that the outdoor pursuits offered by the centre are all mentioned on the licence);
* qualifications and experience of staff;
* any independent recognition or accreditation from bodies such as the British Canoe Union (BCU) or Royal Yachting Association (RYA);
* condition of the equipment;
* first aid provision and accessibility of doctors and hospital.

Try obtaining details of previous users of the centre and contact one or two to discuss their experience. If the centre is unwilling to furnish you with such information, you need to ask yourself (and preferably the centre) why this might be.

Do check the centre's definitions of its responsibility for the supervision of pupils during the visit. It must be clear as to when centre staff will supervise and when teachers will be expected to do so. Never forget that the *duty of care* rests ultimately with the teachers in the party and this is another reason as to why you must satisfy yourself about the suitability of the centre for the proposed learning experiences.

Points to remember

¤ *Planning*

- assess pupils' learning needs, their capabilities, stages of development etc. before setting a clearly related learning focus;
- consider your own knowledge and capabilities and match these to the learning focus and subsequent adventure activities;
- select activities that are related clearly to the proposed learning focus;
- an 'appropriate' activity should be seen as one that matches well the resources of all concerned, i.e. the resources of the learner and the teacher, as well as equipment and environmental resources;
- any piece of equipment must always be utilised for the purpose for which it was originally designed;
- plan to site apparatus and equipment with due regard for pupils' movement onto, across or through, and off the particular piece;
- no activities should be planned that will involve children in chasing, racing or rushing to beat time limits when working off the floor;
- if you elect to use adapted items of equipment or natural resources, it is paramount that you set up and check any proposed arrangement, using appropriate amounts of weight if applicable;
- take a dry run through the activity wherever practically possible as a means to developing a genuine feel for what might occur;
- ensure that pupils will be wearing clothing that allows them to move freely whilst affording suitable protection from the demands of the activity, other pupils or the environment;
- plan to share decisions over safety with the pupils themselves;
- ensure that the lesson format does not place any pressure on you or the children to rush through the planned content; conversely, you don't want the lesson structure to be so loose that pupils drift aimlessly and begin to lose attention;
- plan for subtle variations within the activities themselves to take account of any differing stages of development between the pupils;
- give some thought to the pairings or groupings that will provide for a balanced emotional climate;
- plan to site yourself closer to any group or activity you consider to be higher risk than the rest;
- at each stage of the planning process, conduct a risk assessment and satisfy yourself that no obvious risk is present; consider ways to manage the risk if you wish to retain the activity.

¤ *Teaching*

- two main watchwords – observation and vigilance;
- check over any equipment to be used and also the working area to ensure there are no unwanted obstructions or intrusions;
- teaching position is a paramount consideration within any physical education lesson and you should always feel a sense of contact with each member of the class;
- any adult helpers should be briefed fully on the nature of the activities and any safety considerations, and should be experienced enough to undertake any roles assigned;

- any activities that might involve pupils in supporting each other or working off the ground should be sited in such a way that you are in close contact with them, able to maintain a close eye and able to step in quickly or provide support should it be necessary;
- if at any stage your observations and vigilance cause you to feel uneasy, bring things to a halt in a controlled manner and take time to consider your next move.

¤ *Beyond the school*

- you will be best served if the venture is a clearly planned progression from the work carried out in school;
- satisfy yourself about the suitability of any adult helpers to be used; be assured that they will present no undue risk to your pupils, either in their methods of working or their character, and that they meet the requirements of the school and employer (normally CRB enhanced disclosure certificate);
- a preparatory visit to a local site or an activity centre is essential if you are to assess fully the suitability of the venue and the level of any risk;
- pupils will need to be supervised closely throughout any such visit and if they are to be working in any way that spreads them out as a group, you will have to consider carefully the adult-pupil ratio;
- any equipment within an outside environment should be used for its intended purpose and checked fully; you should consider carefully its appropriateness in helping pupils towards the achievement of particular learning goals;
- talk with staff from a centre prior to any visit; it is best to approach the venture with a good idea about pupils' needs and the ways in which a centre visit might meet these;
- a personal visit is so important because you can develop a feel for the centre as well as being able to check a number of important details;
- check the health and safety policy and code of practice;
- check for public liability insurance;
- check that the centre is in possession of a current licence from the Adventure Activity Licensing Authority (check that the outdoor pursuits offered by the centre are all mentioned on the licence);
- check on the qualifications and experience of the centre staff;
- see if there is any independent recognition or accreditation of the centre from bodies such as the British Canoe Union (BCU) or Royal Yachting Association (RYA);
- try to look at the condition of the centre's equipment;
- satisfy yourself about first aid provision and accessibility of doctors and hospital;
- obtain details of previous users of the centre and contact one or two to discuss their experience;
- check the centre's definitions of its responsibility for the supervision of pupils during the visit; it must be clear as to when centre staff will supervise and when teachers will be expected to do so;
- remember that the duty of care rests ultimately with the teachers in the party.

12 Aquatic activities including swimming and diving

Swimming lessons may take place in school-based pools or local authority operated swimming baths. Although responsibilities may vary according to ownership and operators, in each case the same conditions for effective and safe teaching apply.

Policy documents

All swimming baths sites must (by law) have a *Safety Policy Document*. This, in turn, should include a written *Pool Safety Operating Procedure* (PSOP) consisting of a *Normal Operating Plan* (NOP) and an *Emergency Action Plan* (EAP) covering all pools, changing rooms etc.

Pool Safety Operating Procedure

The PSOP should be available for viewing and should be read by all staff and instructors.

Normal Operating Plan

The NOP should give details of how the pool operates on a daily basis, specific information regarding user groups – such as schools – and any perceived hazards or activity-related risks.

NB Special attention must be given to establishing a routine to ensure that all doors are securely locked when the pool is not in use.

Emergency Action Plan

The EAP should set out – clearly – actions to be taken by staff in the event of an emergency.

Responsibility

The actual teaching of the lesson in LEA schools is usually undertaken by an appropriately qualified instructor (normally possessing an *Amateur Swimming Association (ASA)* or *Swimming Teachers Association (STA) Teachers' certificate*). This in no way absolves the teacher from his or her overall responsibilities and duty of care.

School staff and instructors must be familiar with and fully understand the *Pool Safety Operating Procedure* and should be totally clear as to what to do in case of emergency.

The teacher is *always* responsible for the class and the overall conduct of the lesson, and any instructor or seconded lifeguard works *under the authority of the teacher*. The teacher may take an *active teaching* role in the lesson as agreed with the instructor, for example working with a group of pupils, or alternatively may take a more passive role as an observer.

The teacher, in either role, must appreciate that he or she is always part of the operational team. He or she should continuously observe the whole class regardless of whether he or she is teaching all or a number of the pupils or has a non-teaching role. Those observed must include pupils who may be present but are not taking part in the activities.

The teacher must *never leave the pool* or spend time talking, at any length, to any other adult or child.

Two pools may be used only if both are clearly visible to the class teacher.

The buddy system

The '*buddy system*' with pupils paired off at the beginning of the lesson, each being made responsible, at all times, for reporting if the other is in difficulties, should *never be used*. Pupils, rightly, become absorbed in what they are doing and cannot be expected to concentrate on checking other pupils at the same time as they are working.

When working alternately in pairs (one in and one out of the water, changing over periodically) pupils can be asked to focus on their partners and report if they are seen to be in difficulties. This does not absolve the staff of their responsibilities for surveillance.

Responsibility in an emergency

One member of staff will be designated the leader in case of emergencies. Although the teacher will still be responsible for the class, it may make sense for the instructor to act as the leader, as he or she may be more familiar with the buildings and procedures.

Life saving qualifications and life-guards

At least one of the staff present should be fully conversant with pool rescue and cardio-pulmonary resuscitation techniques and hold an appropriate minimum qualification (normally a Royal Life Saving Society (RLSS) bronze medallion or Lifeguard award). The qualification must be re-taken every 2–3 years. This person can be the teacher, the instructor or a lifeguard employed by the pool who is in attendance throughout the lesson.

If a lifeguard is to be provided by a local authority or private pool, this must be agreed in the contract made by the LEA or the school.

Basic safety points

Routines should be developed and always adhered to for all aspects of the lesson, including any use of transport to a pool.

Both pupils and staff must be fully aware of, and regularly practise, what to do in emergency situations, including evacuation of the pool, as laid down in the EAP.

The teacher should be able to *see* and *hear* all the children and the children the teacher in all phases of the lesson, including transportation to the pool.

Pupil to teacher ratio

Determining the *maximum number of pupils* that may be taken by one or more teachers and/or instructors, possibly with qualified back-up, is of absolutely vital importance.

BAALPE, in *Safe Practice in Physical Education* (1999), state

> As circumstances and the building design of a swimming pool vary greatly, it is not possible to give a definitive set of ratios.

They go on to point out that a policy must be based on a thorough risk assessment and specified local requirements that '*must take precedence*'.

Vitally important factors that must be taken into consideration are:

- the age and ability levels of the pupils taking part in the lesson;
- the actual conditions, including floor depth and gradient and the shape and setting of the pool;
- whether the pool is being shared with members of the public and in what way;
- how many children with special educational needs or medical conditions are in the class.

Competency

In the ASA-endorsed document, *Safe Supervision for Teaching and Coaching Swimming*, the basic recommended ratio (i.e. not to be exceeded) is *20:1*. This refers to what the ASA term *improving swimmers* (able to swim competently on front and back unaided for at least 10 metres) and *competent swimmers* (as above, but for 25 metres, plus being able to tread water for two minutes). It also applies to mixed groups – with the very important proviso that the least able and less confident are *well within their depth* and the improvers are confined to an area that is within their depth.

Although the optimum ratio would depend on a number of factors, including swimmer competence at whatever activity is being done, it might be useful to consider 20:1 as a 'benchmark' i.e. not to be exceeded. Adjustments would be made according to the overall composition of a class or group, with the ratio possibly being reduced if there are a high number of absolute beginners and/or poor swimmers requiring a high level of attention.

Pupils with special needs

Depending on the total numbers in the class and the aptitude of the children, the presence of pupils with special needs (including those with physical disabilities) may mean that ratios have to be reduced.

An 'additional pair of eyes'

Following a well-publicised drowning in a school lesson, many authorities adopted the 'two pairs of eyes' rule. This meant that there always had to be at least two adults for a designated number of pupils, usually between 20 and 24, with a further two adults required for any additional numbers up to 40 or 48, and so on. Although excellent in regard to safe practice, with standard classes of around 30 requiring four qualified or responsible adults present at each lesson the demands on schools in regard to teachers, and pools in regard to lifeguards, proved to be too great and the system was gradually replaced with options which were more practicable.

However, the principle of having two responsible adults present for each lesson is an excellent one, allowing much better surveillance and, importantly, for one to remain with the children if the other is involved in an emergency operation. This fits with the standard practice of a teacher working in tandem with a swimming instructor.

In certain circumstances other qualified adults may be required. For example, if there are particular problems with visibility, mobility round the pool edge, range of activities, or number and composition of groups (particularly if including SEN pupils) and their operating areas.

NB Lifeguards employed at the pool may be seconded to fulfil this role providing they work *exclusively* with the class.

¤ *Summary of recommendations for safe pupil to teacher ratios*

- There should always be a minimum of two responsible adults with each class, one of whom is suitably qualified in rescue techniques and life saving.
- A *maximum* ratio of 20:1 should be the norm for pupils of this age.
- A lower ratio of non-swimmers and beginners per teacher/instructor may be considered. This would allow the teacher to give more individual attention to each child at this stage of his or her learning. This essential help and feedback leads to increased confidence and lower stress levels resulting in quicker water adjustment and, ultimately, swimming stroke development. The greater the confidence the greater the awareness and the safer the practice becomes.
- If there are a high number of non-swimmers (say more than 12), they should be split into two groups. If there is sufficient space for the children to operate in comfort and two teachers are available, the groups can work in parallel. If shallow water space is limited and/or numbers are high, each group must work for half the time available, one following the other, until a sufficient number of children reach levels of competence to allow all the children to work at the same time.
- A reduction in the ratios must be considered when
  - the general public is present and share the same operating areas and/or
  - SEN pupils are in the class.

  Depending on the number of pupils present, this could mean halving the ratios stated above.
- Where conditions demand it (for example, pool design, public sharing, activity range or larger numbers well in excess of 30) another adult may be required. This may be a teacher or class assistant fully aware of the nature of the duty, or a lifeguard paying sole attention to the class.
- A maximum of 12 foundation and very young KS1 pupils may be assisted by parents (or adults nominated by the parents) to become acclimatised to the water, prior to eventually working unaided on a structured programme.
- Any adults assisting in the water are under the control of the teacher in charge and, when present, the qualified instructor.

NB If the teacher considers that ratios suggested by instructors are too high, then a request must be made to reduce them. If this is not acceded to, the pupils may have to be withdrawn from the lesson and the head teacher asked to take up the matter with the instructor's employers. Safety is the most important factor.

Prior preparation

Eating

Pupils *must not eat* a meal or any form of solid food within an absolute minimum of one hour before entering the pool. A longer time span is desirable but not always possible. There is a case on record of a girl of junior school age who went swimming immediately after eating a full lunch. She struck her head on the tiled edge when entering the water and lost consciousness. Although she was pulled out immediately and given resuscitation by the baths manager, regurgitated food blocked the windpipe and could not be cleared. Air was prevented from entering the lungs and, despite being taken immediately to the hospital that was adjacent to the pool, the girl unfortunately died.

Teachers must constantly check that no sandwiches, chocolate bars or other food items are eaten in transit or in the changing rooms. This is absolutely vital.

Pre-instruction

Before going swimming for the first time, pupils should be informed of the pool conditions (particularly depths), what they will be expected to do in the pool, and the routines employed prior to entering the pool.

This will be reinforced, in stages, when the pupils actually go. Reminders may also be necessary in subsequent weeks.

Fitness to participate

Each week, the teacher must check to ensure that the pupils are medically fit to take an active part in the lesson. This should be done prior to leaving the classroom or school premises.

Skin conditions

Skin conditions are a particular concern. Pupils who develop spots, rashes or eczema. should not be allowed to take part unless they have medical evidence to show that the condition is not contagious or will not affect or be affected by the water in any way.

Cuts and sores

Pupils with unhealed cuts or open sores, even when covered with elastoplasts, would not normally be allowed to swim. Similarly, any child wearing a bandage would not normally be allowed to swim, unless this can be made totally waterproof.

Colds and infections

Pupils with coughs, colds, catarrh, sinusitis, sore eyes or ear infections should not be allowed to take part.

Verrucas

Verrucas should be covered over when at the poolside but not necessarily in the water.

Other conditions

There are a number of conditions (e.g. epilepsy, asthma, diabetes, temporary or ongoing joint problems) that may not prevent a child from participating but should be taken into account when planning lesson material and anticipating what action may be required in case of emergencies. Advice from, or discussion with parents and/or medical advisers, may either be necessary or of great help.

Procedures at the pool

Counting pupils

It is absolutely essential that pupils be *counted* – on and off the coach, into the premises, on entering the pool area, on leaving the pool, on leaving the premises, and again when getting on and off the coach. This routine was not carried out on one occasion at a school-based pool and a pupil remained behind – locked in – over the lunch break. She went back into the water and was drowned.

Routine

Pupils must follow a routine for changing and entering the pool.

Hygiene

The children should conform to any hygiene procedures that are laid down (use handkerchief, visit toilet, shower, foot bath etc.). Although these are not specific safety measures, they do help establish a set pattern that underpins sensible, and therefore safe, behaviour.

Eating

Pupils must not eat sweets or chew gum during any phase of the lesson.

Assembly at pool-side

Pupils should *walk* to a designated area, away from the pool edge, and wait quietly until instructions for work in the water are given.

Pupil behaviour at the pool

Pupils must *never*:

- *enter* or *leave* the pool area or the water without permission from the class teacher or instructor. It should be made clear to the pupils that no one else has the authority to give permission;
- run anywhere in the pool area;

- chase each other, in or out of the water;
- push or trip other pupils on the pool surrounds;
- jump or dive into the water, unless given express permission to do so or the activities are part of the lesson content.

Goggles

Adjusting the position of goggles is an ongoing distraction. Therefore, pupils should only be allowed to wear them if they have eye problems.

¤ Pool safety and operating conditions

At least one of the adults present, qualified in rescue techniques, should be prepared to enter the water and wear appropriate clothes in order to do so.

Life saving and first aid equipment

Life saving equipment must be readily available and clearly visible. There should be apparatus that can be used to assist pupils who are experiencing difficulties, fatigue etc. For example, buoyancy aids (possibly attached to a rope) or long poles.

Teachers should be aware of the position of (a) any alarm bell designed to alert additional help and (b) a telephone to be used in emergencies.

There should be first aid equipment and a suitable stretcher and blanket available. Teachers should check to ensure that the life saving and first aid equipment is actually there.

The emergency and first aid equipment and alarms etc. should be checked daily. In local authority baths, this is the responsibility of the manager. At school-based sites either the head teacher or an LEA employee, as agreed by the authority, is responsible. (The actual daily checking may be done by a caretaker, pool attendant or instructor.)

Signage

Pool depths and danger areas (including 'no-go' areas) should be indicated on walls, using the correct European standards design, and brought to the attention of pupils.

Pool dividers

A pool divider of a suitable type should be laid across the water surface to 'partition' off the shallow water area to be used by non-swimmers (see *In the water* and Figure 12.1).

Line of sight

Teachers and instructors must be able to *easily see the pool bottom* over the whole of the working area. Therefore,

- the water should be clean;
- if affected by surface glare from sun or artificial light, new teaching positions must be taken up.

Disinfectant

In order to prevent inflammation of the eyes, the prescribed level of disinfectant must not be exceeded. Pupils, possibly the whole class, should leave the pool if there is evidence of distress.

Temperature

Water temperature should ideally be a minimum of 28°C. If all are able to swim and keep moving in the water, it is possible to operate at slightly lower temperatures.

Air temperature should be slightly above that of the water.

Cold water and air are dangerous. They cause stress and, as children focus on the coldness and shivering, they are distracted from the prescribed tasks and the teacher. Attempting to work in cold water can be counter-productive, accentuating fear and working against long-term development and safe practice.

Surfaces

Broken edge tiles or cracked surfaces should be repaired as quickly as possible and cordoned off until this has been done.

If a surface has been found to be slippery (through wear or using the wrong cleaning material), the affected area must be partitioned off or, if affecting the whole pool, the lesson may have to be delayed, until cleaning is undertaken, or even abandoned. Risks must not be taken!

¤ Class organisation

The class can operate safely as a whole or split into groups (as would more normally be the case in the later Key stages).

Careful checks on ability should be made when a class first goes to a pool and when new pupils first enter the water. Records of progress should be kept.

Teaching in groups

After initial checks on ability, pupils would then be placed in groups (usually three, although four is possible). Depending on the standards already reached, the pupils would be divided as follows:

*   non-swimmers, beginners and basic swimmers;
    or
*   non-swimmers and beginners together, improvers and competent swimmers.

A teacher or instructor may take the whole class or work with one or more groups. Any other groups would be taken by the other member of staff. If two or more groups are taken by one person, then, even when instructions are being given to one set of children, attention must be constantly given to the members of any other group under his or her control. The teacher should also keep checking pupils who are not in the water.

Pool sharing

Particular vigilance is required when members of the public are sharing the use of the pool. If possible, areas should be sectioned off for exclusive use by the school.

If the public also use the pool and there is a diving board, no activities should take place in the immediate vicinity of the board.

Assistance in the water

It is recommended that instructors and teachers do *not* get into the water to 'assist' pupils. When learning water skills, assistance of this kind is of very doubtful value. Many pupils may become stressed because they feel that the right to make decisions has been taken away from them. They may not have developed the necessary confidence levels to attempt a particular movement and being 'pushed' is seen as a form of coercion.

In causing tension and, often, rapid breathing, the pupils become less perceptive and focused and, therefore, more prone to get into difficulties. The adult in the water is focusing on one child and, being at water level, is in a much poorer position to check on others. The onus for surveillance is then entirely on the other adult present.

If such in-water assistance is deemed to be of value, it should be provided by a responsible adult who operates in addition to those maintaining supervision on the poolside (a minimum of two).

Observation

Teachers should position themselves so that they are in the best position to observe the pupils working (either the whole class or groups, depending on the form of supervision) and should keep returning to this position after giving instructions. This may mean taking a diagonal rather than a head-on viewing position.

If the lesson is taking place in a modern leisure pool which is an irregular shape, has different areas for different purposes (possibly of different depths), or has pillars obstructing the view, the teacher must

- ensure the class or group can be observed from one position or, if that is not possible;
- keep changing position so that all pupils are continually being seen.

If neither of these is possible, and, in the absence of additional staff, the pupils will have to be divided into smaller sub-groups that can be seen all the time and share the time available.

Avoiding the pool edge

Pupils should not queue or line up along the edge of the pool, particularly if the water is deep.

Slides, diving boards and wave machines

Pupils should not be allowed to use slides or diving boards or stand in waves made by a machine.

¤ In the water

Entering and leaving the pool

Pupils must enter and exit the pool by a taught method, either from a sitting position on the pool edge or, in file, down steps.

Partitions

As stated, where non-swimmers and beginners are using the 'shallow-end' of a standard pool, the area where it is safe for them to operate should be partitioned off using a pool divider (see Figure 12.1).

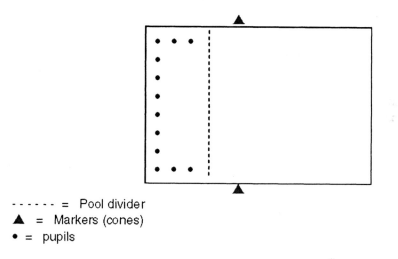

- - - - - - = Pool divider
▲ = Markers (cones)
• = pupils

Figure 12.1 Pool dividers and markers

NB Ideally, there should be demarcation of the areas in which other groups of pupils are operating.

For improvers and competent swimmers, this can be done by using more pool dividers or by placing cones on the edge. If cones are used, teachers need to check regularly that they have not been moved and that the pupils stay within the prescribed areas.

Buoyancy aids

The wearing of buoyancy aids does *not* make it safe for poor and non-swimmers to operate in deep water.

Clear pathways in the pool

Teachers and instructors should check to ensure that there is a clear path for the pupils before they begin each width, length or continuous unit of swimming. This is particularly important when swimming on the back and sharing the pool with the public.

Noise

Noise levels can be a problem and pupils should be taught to work quietly so that teachers can be heard. Given that shared use and pool buildings often accentuate noise, a simple system of communication should be established. *Whistles* can be very valuable, particularly when the pool has other activity areas or there is a general hubbub of noise. For example,

One whistle –   In shallow water, stop and stand still; return to the edge on command.
            In deeper water, continue crossing and stop at the edge.
Two whistles –   Get out of the pool using the established method.

Teaching non-swimmers

In theory, provided the conditions are right, the method used to teach swimming should not affect the safety. In practice, it can make an appreciable difference.

It is recommended that beginners undertake a full programme of confidence work, including preliminary 'drownproofing' activities, prior to attempting swimming. The resulting absence of muscle tension, breathing problems and feelings of apprehension combined with the ability to go under the water without fear, leads to learning strokes more easily and, often, with better technique. As a result of their increased confidence, pupils can operate with less discomfort and risk of accidents.

Only when pupils have *fully* demonstrated that they have the capability to progress should they move on to new practices and/or a different environment. It is very easy to 'push' too soon.

Lesson form

Lesson form can vary according to ability and need.

It is not recommended that pupils are allowed a period of *free play* at the end of the lesson; *free choice* possibly, where they practise skills learned in that or previous lessons. Free play encourages inter-pupil contact, daring methods of entry and use of pool equipment and, in so doing, increases the possibility of accidents.

Limitations

*   Demands should always be matched to the pupils' abilities.
*   Swimming at high speed should be kept to short time spans and rest periods always interspersed.
*   Strict limitations on distance swimming should be imposed, according to capability. Time limits should not be imposed or pressure to swim quickly brought to bear.

Diving

A very useful rule of thumb, still advocated by the ASA in its guidance on teaching diving, is that pupils should only dive into water of a depth that exceeds the distance between their feet and their fingertips when arms are fully stretched and raised vertically above the head. This allows a great deal of scope for primary school pupils to dive into the deep end of 'standard' pools.

In shallow water teaching pools, there is a great deal of preliminary work that can be done from starting positions in the water.

It is recommended that:

- diving is never allowed in any type of shallow water i.e. in a teaching pool or the shallow end of a standard pool;
- diving may be taught in a pool with a 'deep end', provided that the teaching is undertaken by a person who has taken an appropriate course covering technique and lead-up activities;
- pupils are not allowed to dive in a free choice period unless given specific permission to do so by the instructor or other qualified person who has observed the pupil in practice;
- no diving be undertaken from boards in any part of the swimming baths area;
- if the water depth is only just greater than the full stretch finger tip height of the taller pupils, it may be deemed safer to limit dives to those with starting positions in which the head and upper body are closer to the water (e.g. adopting a piked or crouch position or placing one knee on the side alongside one foot).

Pupils with disabilities

The teacher or instructor or a trained assistant should, if required, know how to

- assist pupils from the changing rooms and into and out of the water;
- give support in the water – both for static positions and to aid movement;
- know exactly how to operate a hoist if there is one in the pool.

Special floats may be required. These are larger than normal, providing easy hand-holds, or adapted so that they can be attached to the body safely and provide a very stable position.

Medical conditions

In addition to the general points made in chapter 2, it may be necessary to ascertain whether pupils with certain medical conditions have any particular needs in regard to undertaking water activities. For example,

- specific restrictions;
- personal help in the water or through observation;
- additional food to be taken up to an hour before;
- liquids, food or medicine at the poolside;
- action to be taken in the event of any problem occurring.

Special needs pupils

Instructions may have to be made doubly clear and checks carried out to ensure that these instructions have been understood. A very close watch should be kept throughout.

Additional information

It is recommended that all pool operators should have the manual, *Managing Health and Safety in Swimming Pools*, jointly published by the HSC and Sport England.

¤ Checklist of major points for safe swimming

- Pupils should always be medically fit to participate.
- Pupils must never eat any foods within an absolute minimum of one hour before entering the pool. Pupils must not eat sweets or chew gum during the activity period.
- Pupils should be counted at different stages of the visit to the pool.
- Every pool should have an Emergency Action Plan as part of a Safety Policy Document. Teachers and instructors must be familiar with its contents and understand what to do in emergencies. One person should be designated the leader in regard to emergency action.
- The class teacher retains overall responsibility for the class at all times.
- Pupils must be aware of all procedures, including emergency routines for clearing the pool and buildings, and risks covering all aspects of the visit to the baths.
- Pupils should periodically practise emergency procedures.
- All pools should have a full complement of first aid and rescue equipment.
- At least one adult present should have up-to-date qualifications in first aid, resuscitation and rescue techniques.
- Pupils should be made aware of pool depths at different points.
- Pupils should be taught procedures for getting in and out of the water and stopping work.
- A pool divider should be used to 'contain' non-swimmers and beginners in shallow water.
- Recommended maximum ratios for beginners and swimmers should not be exceeded.
- It is recommended that teachers and instructors do not enter the water, except in case of emergencies. There should *always* be two responsible adults on the poolside.
- Lesson content should be closely matched to pupils' abilities.
- No pupil should ever be subjected to coercion.
- The responsibility for checking children in the water should never be left to other pupils.

NB Particular attention should be paid to those paragraphs above concerned with procedures, both prior to going to the pool and on the premises, including those dealing with emergencies.

Appendix A – Health-related exercise

Knowledge and understanding of fitness and health is a statutory requirement of each Key Stage. By the time they have finished Key Stage 2, pupils are expected to have some understanding of the effects of exercise.

Activities may be, largely, divided into two areas, those that can be seen as dual purpose (i.e. recognised units of a given activity such as games or athletics which also contribute to fitness development), and those which are discrete and relate specifically to elements such as strength, flexibility and stamina.

The same rules regarding safe environmental conditions and the use of apparatus and equipment, outlined in the previous chapters, apply. There are, however, additional safeguards that apply to exercises and activities designed to specifically improve flexibility, stamina and strength. Teachers should be aware of them.

Children up to the age of eleven are not yet ready for sustained or repetitive exercises or lifting or carrying of heavy objects, and long-term damage can result if they are attempted.

The most important general and specific points are listed below.

¤ Guidelines for warming up and cooling down

Children of this age rarely, if ever, pull muscles, and there are physiologists who argue that there is no need for pupils to do specific warm-ups until they are older. However, there are many physical educationalists and NGBs of sport who advocate warming up and cooling down in each lesson in order to inculcate good habits.

The NC states that pupils must gain knowledge of the purpose and principles of warming up and cooling down.

- The same golden rules that are listed in the *Checklist of major points for safe health-related exercise* apply to warming up and cooling down.
- The class should always work together but individuals be allowed to match activities and number and rate of repetitions to their own abilities. No one should feel fatigued.
- There should be no competitive aspect to the warm-up or cool-down.
- There should be gradual progression. Where applicable, slow movements should precede quick actions (e.g. jogging easily in and out, followed by gradual acceleration runs; never flat-out sprints at the start).
- Material that is both part of or related to the main lesson content and suitable for warming up is ideal.

¤ **Checklist of major points for safe health-related exercise (including warming up and cooling down)**

- Avoid prolonged *full effort* exercise such as running and swimming over long distances, e.g. no racing over distances greater than 100 metres in athletics.
- Avoid sustained high-intensity effort, such as repeated double foot jumps or hops.
- Avoid *repeated* deep knee bending, as in jumps (particularly down from boxes and benches) or in 'duck' movements or competitions. Bunny jumps can be practised in gymnastics but there must be reasonable periods of rest between each set of attempts.
- There should be no stretching while bouncing on the feet.
- No specific 'adult type' strength building exercises such as full press-ups should be attempted. The emphasis in KS2 should be on skill and there is no need to include specific strength building work. If such activities are included they should be heavily modified (e.g. semi-vertical press-ups against a wall) and allow for a wide range in capacity.
- Weights and machines should not be used in primary schools.
- Pupils should not be expected to do 'fitness training' designed to improve stamina for events in athletics or swimming. Too many young children are over-worked at too early a point in swimming, putting them under physiological strain and, also, incidentally, often destroying motivation.
- Many exercises that have been regularly used in the past to mobilise joints or stretch muscles are now believed to be dangerous (e.g. touching toes from standing with straight legs) and should be avoided. Safe alternatives should now be used, possibly as part of a warm-up (e.g. bent-knee as opposed to straight leg sit-ups).
- Exercises that involve extremes of stretching or arching or bending can result in long-term damage and should be avoided.
- Exercises and movements must be performed correctly, e.g. with the correct degree of knee bend in landing, on the balls of the feet, etc.
- Stretching should be done by moving gently into a position and holding still for a few seconds, never by swinging the limbs violently and/or taking up the most extreme position.
- Muscles should be warm before they are stretched.

A comprehensive guide to recommended stretches, exercises that are considered unsafe plus alternatives, strength building etc. and how to safely incorporate this material into warm-ups, cooling down and other parts of lessons can be found in the book *Teaching Health-Related Exercise at Key Stages 1 and 2* (see Appendix F).

Appendix B – Playground markings

Figure B.1 represents both a recommended lay-out and a number of alternative ideas for playground markings.

The markings are extremely useful in regard to creating ready-made areas for a large variety of activities with built-in safety. Lines and symbols will be painted, the vast majority in white and a number in another acceptable colour such as yellow.

- There should always be a large basic rectangle. Size may vary according to playground dimensions and shape.

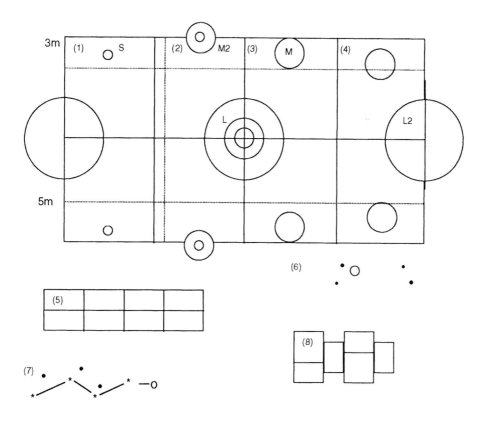

Figure B.1 Basic rectangle and ideas for marking

- This rectangle is divided into eight equal-sized smaller rectangles. This grid enables basic group work to take place (for example, seven or eight groups of four).
- Pairs of basic rectangles can be combined to give four larger areas, (1), (2), (3) and (4), with longer sides. Four- or five-a-side games, such as skittle ball can be played in these. An alternative is to create a netball court, subdividing each of the three sectors into two, giving six basic rectangles.
- A further line, either dotted or a different colour, can be painted 1 or 2 metres inside the left hand side of each long rectangle (illustrated in (2)), allowing a space to be left between each five-a-side game.
- The large, medium and small circles give opportunity for a large range of activities, many based on passing.
- The large semi-circles, as in L2, could match the netball Ds and, also, provide a protected area in other activities using small goals, including those *attack vs defence* practices where either one group is always attempting to score and the other, generally smaller in number, is aiming to stop them (e.g. 3 vs 2) or teams of equal numbers with both taking up attacking and defensive roles according to which is in possession of the ball.
- The 3 and 1 metre circles, as shown by M and S, can be selected according to the size that is required and whether, in a game, players may operate round the whole circumference. For example, in (2), the 3 metre circle can provide a 'protection' area for a goalkeeper and, in (4), in allowing movement round the whole perimeter, the positioning is ideal for games like skittle ball.
- The 3 and 5 metre dotted lines create markings and positions for net-type activities (see Appendix C, *Group work*).
- The markings outside the basic rectangle can be positioned according to playground shape. They allow for activities that do not require contained areas. (5), (7) and (8) provide a variety of dribbling and agility circuits with markers placed on lines, intersections or symbols or in spaces as appropriate (e.g. in (7) the *s provide an easy route, the mixture of *s and •s a more difficult challenge). (5), (6) and (8) provide targets for throwing beanbags or quoits or bouncing balls (with the circle in (6) being either marked or a moveable hoop and the dots pairs of pupils), (8) for hopscotch etc.
- The whole is ideal for setting up relays of different kinds with markers placed on the various lengthways lines as appropriate.

The whole makes for easy and thus safer setting up of activities and distribution of equipment.

Appendix C – Group work

One of the main purposes of group work is to allow a range of different activities to be experienced in one lesson. Limited numbers of pieces of apparatus which could not be made available to the whole class at the same time (e.g. badminton posts used to stretch a net across at different heights and widths for rolling balls under or throwing or hitting over) can also be brought into play.

- The distance between each group should be based on the nature of each of the adjacent activities and should allow for any possible movement outside a designated area that may occur as a result of the activity.
- Some activities are 'self-contained' by their nature, while others require demarcation. Operating areas may be bounded by painted lines and/or cones and/or marker domes or even ropes or beanbags.
- The siting of each activity should take into account the possible practice outcomes. If balls are being struck, it should be in an 'open' direction i.e. where there are no children operating. Also, it should not be in close proximity to a road or area where other people may be hit.
- Practices are organised to minimise the possibility of balls constantly flying across the playground.
- Any posts connected by a net should have sufficiently heavy bases or weighting systems to prevent them being pulled over if a child tangles with the net.
- The example, shown in Figure C.1, is a mixture of small apparatus, games practices and games. It is designed for graded groups of four in lower to middle KS2 but could easily be 'converted' to activities suitable for upper KS2. The areas bounding the activities could, as suggested above, be based on painted playground markings or a netball court with added chalked lines and/or marker domes (see *Appendix B – Playground Markings*).

Suggested Activities

Activity i

Hitting a ball with wooden or plastic bats over a low net or bench. The playing area can vary according to practice or game and ability. Rubber and tennis balls can be used to develop 'cooperation' volleying etc. and airflows, which do not 'fly', for games. The ball, if missed, would tend to run into free space at one end and past activity (ii) at the other.

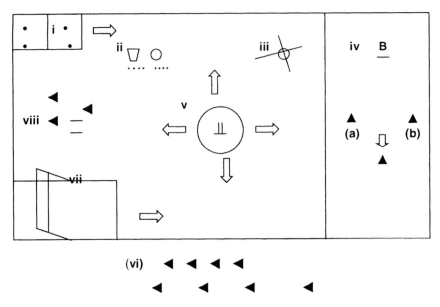

Figure C.1 Suggested group work lay-out

Activity ii

Target work using beanbags and bins or hoops that is fairly self-contained. (NB Any poor catchers can practise with the beanbag not rolling away.)

Activity iii

In pairs, bouncing small balls into a hoop using different types of throw, different distances etc. Angles can be used that minimise the chances of the ball interfering with other groups.

Activity iv

This is a striking activity. The direction is tightly controlled as the ball must be hit between the two cones (a) and (b) and into 'free' space beyond that with the batter attempting to run round the cones before the fielders can retrieve the ball and perform some task with it (throw and catch, roll etc.). If there is a problem regarding residential housing, roads or other dangers, the ball may be rolled or bounced out or hit onto the ground.

Activity v

Large ball passing activities across the circle or tower ball – attempting to hit a cone protected by one of the children. The ball can bounce in different directions but performers in the two nearest activities, (ii) and (iii), are static and there is a reasonable distance between this and the other activities.

Activity vi

A ball is dribbled by hand, foot or stick between markers matched to ability.

Activity vii

A net is suspended across appropriate, properly anchored posts e.g. badminton. A ball is thrown over the net to be caught and thrown back. It develops into a very dynamic game, each pair trying to outwit the other and get the ball to bounce on the court on the opponents' side of the net. This could also be battington, badminton or head tennis. The siting is very safe with the ball, if missed, moving into free space and down the unused section of the playground or field.

Activity viii

Skipping development, from basic on the spot to moving round a small circuit using a variety of styles.

Activities (i) (3 metres width), (iv) (a full width rectangle), (v) (a centre circle), (vi) (off-court dribble markings) and (vii) (5 metres width) could be set up using the type of playground markings shown in Appendix B.

NB *Potted Sports*, in which balanced teams compete against each other in a range of athletics and games types skills, is a form of group work. Information is given in chapter 10, *Athletics, Potted sports*.

Appendix D – Goalpost safety guidelines

Extract from chapter VII, *Health and Safety*, in the *Football Curriculum Guide* (FA in conjunction with the PEAUK, 2000).

Goalpost safety guidelines

The Football Association, along with the Department for Culture, Media and Sport, the Health and Safety Executive and the British Standards Institution, would like to draw your attention to the following guidelines for the safe use of goalposts. Too many serious injuries and fatalities have occurred in recent years as a result of unsafe or incorrect use of goalposts. Safety is always of paramount importance and everyone in football must play their part to prevent similar incidents occurring in the future.

1. For safety reasons goalposts of any size (including those that are portable and not installed permanently at a pitch or practice field) must always be anchored securely to the ground.

   - Portable goalposts must be secured by use of chain anchors or appropriate anchor weights to prevent them from toppling forward.
   - It is essential that under no circumstances should children or adults be allowed to climb, swing on or play with the structures of the goalposts.
   - Particular attention is drawn to the fact that if not properly assembled and secured, portable goalposts may topple over.
   - Regular inspections of goalposts should be carried out to check that they are kept properly maintained.

2. Portable goalposts should not be left in place after use. They should be dismantled and removed to a place of secure storage.

3. It is strongly recommended that nets should only be secured by plastic hooks or tape and not by metal cup hooks. Any metal cup hooks should if possible be removed and replaced. New goalposts should not be purchased if they include metal cup hooks which cannot be replaced.

4. Goalposts which are 'home made' or which have been altered from their original size or construction should not be used. These have been the cause of a number of deaths and injuries.

5. Guidelines to prevent toppling:

   i. Follow manufacturer's guidelines in assembling posts.
  ii. Before use, adults should:

- ensure each goal is anchored securely in its place;
- exert a significant downward force on the crossbar;
- exert a significant backward force on both upright posts;
- exert a significant forward force on both upright posts.

This must be repeated until it is established that the structure is secure. If not, alternative goals/pitches must be used.

Appendix E – Trampoline

Trampolining is normally conducted with a number of spotters round the frame (a minimum of one along each side or end) or, much more rarely, a combination of spotters and appropriately placed mattresses. The system, designed to prevent children coming off the bed and hitting the hard metal edges or landing on the floor, depends on the ability of each spotter to push anyone who has lost control back onto the bed.

NB Children of primary age are not physically capable of doing this.

Therefore, in order for trampolining to take place, it would be necessary to have either

- four mature and experienced spotters who can be trusted to push children back when required;
  or
- a combination of correctly positioned safety mattresses of sufficient thickness and mature competent spotters (standing at the sides that are not covered with mattresses).

There is also a risk of injury, possibly severe, if children attempt movements on the trampoline that they have not been taught or make mistakes when learning those that have been prescribed. It is therefore essential that a teacher or instructor who has an up-to-date British Gymnastics or British Trampoline Federation (now part of British Gymnastics) trampoline coaching certificate and experience of working with children of this age and understands their needs in regard to progression and safe practice is responsible for the lesson content.

NB Given the inherent dangers in working on trampolines at this age, the difficulty in finding up to four responsible spotters and the fact that it is hard to justify on educational grounds (with just one child on a trampoline at one time, the others waiting their turns), it is strongly recommended that trampoline activities should *not* be included in primary school physical education programmes.

For more information on the trampoline, refer to *Safe Practice in Physical Education* (BAALPE).

Appendix F – Sources of information, useful contacts, bibliography and references

Recommended for ALL Schools

BAALPE (British Association of Advisers and Lecturers in PE) (1979; fifth edition 1999) *Safe Practice in Physical Education.* (New edition every 4–5 years.)

BAALPE (1989; second edition 1996) *Physical Education for Pupils with Special Educational Needs in Mainstream Education.* Contact General Secretary, BAALPE, Sports Development Centre, Loughborough University, Loughborough, Leicestershire, LE11 3TU.

Recommended for schools responsible for the maintenance of

Gymnastics and outdoor play apparatus

SAFEA (Sports and Fitness Equipment Association) (1997) *Guidance.* British Sports and Allied Industries Federation. Gives advice to contractors and clients (schools, LEAs) regarding the inspection and repairs of physical education and sports equipment in schools.

Games and athletics equipment

SAFEA (2001) *SAFEA and Safe Play Recommended Maintenance Guidelines for Outdoor Sports and Athletics Equipment.* The Sports Industries Federation. Gives advice on fixed games and athletics equipment.

Both the above booklets are available free of charge from: SAFEA, Federation House, National Agricultural Centre, Stoneleigh Park, Warwickshire CV8 2RF.

Swimming pools

HSC and Sport England (1988 as *Safety in Swimming Pools*; second edition 1999) *Managing Health and Safety in Swimming Pools.* HSC and Sport England (see below).

Information, contacts and references

Activity and sport specific

Many national governing bodies of sports and associated bodies now produce their own material on teaching/coaching and health and safety. All can be contacted for further help, including guidance on equipment.

Association football

FA and PEAUK (1995; second edition 2000) *Football Curriculum Guide*. FA Ltd, PO Box HP86, Leeds, LS6 3XW.

Athletics

UK Athletics (2000) *Approved Code of Practice: The Safe Conduct of Track and Field Events*. 30A Harborne Road, Edgebaston, Birmingham, B15 3AA.

ESAA (2001) *Handbook*. Hon. Sec. 26 Newborough Green, New Malden, Surrey KT3 5HS. Information on recommended specifications and safety.

Bunner, G. (1984; third edition 1995) *The Sports Hall Athletics Manual*. Sports Hall Athletics Association from G. Bunner, Unit 8, Duttons Business Centre, Dock Road, Northwich, Cheshire, CW9 5HJ. Information on events that can be done indoors, in some cases in school halls, by Years 4–6, with a stress on safe practice.

Basketball

Mini-Basketball England *Mini-Basketball Guidelines* PO Box 22, Royston, Hertfordshire, SG8 5NB. Includes an excellent section on safety and first aid.

Cricket

ECB *Howzat: Playing the Game (KS2)*. ECB, Cricket Dept. Lords, London, NW8 8QZ. All counties have development officers who will visit schools on request.

Gymnastics

British Gymnastics (2001) *Health, Safety and Welfare Policy for Coaches and Clubs*. British Gymnastics, Ford Hall, Lilleshall National Sports Centre, Newport, Shropshire TF10 9NB. A very comprehensive document covering safety and risk with sections on coaching, equipment, and child protection.

National Primary Centre (1993) *Let's Move Apparatus (KS1 and 2)*. Birmingham City Council Education Department. Birmingham City Council Advisory and Support Service, Martineau Centre, Balden Road, Harborne, Birmingham B32 2EH. A very useful video and accompanying booklet.

Life saving

RLSS (Royal Life Saving Society UK), River House, High Street, Broom, Warwickshire, B50 4HN.

Netball

All England Netball Association (1999) *Duty of Care Guidelines for Netball*. AENA, Netball House, 9 Paynes Park, Hitchin, Hertfordshire, SG5 1EH.

Rugby

Rugby Football Union, Rugby Road, Twickenham, Middlesex, TW1 1DS. Information available on a variety of aspects including New Image Rugby, safety, codes of practice and child protection.

Softball

Baseball/Softball UK, Ariel House, 74a Charlotte Street, London, W1P 1LR. Information available on safety and recommended dimensions.

Swimming

Amateur Swimming Association, Institute of Sport and Recreation Managers, Institute of Swimming Teachers and Coaches and the Royal Life Saving Society (1996) *Safe Supervision for Teaching and Coaching Swimming.*

Amateur Swimming Association (1998) *Swimming Teaching and Coaching (Level 1).* Swimming Times. Both available from ASA, Harold Fern House, Derby Square, Loughborough, Leicestershire, LE11 5AL.

Background information

British Standards Institution (BSI) 389 Chiswick High Road, London, W4 4AL.

Medical and first aid

DfEE *Guidance on First Aid for Schools.* Available free of charge from DfES Publications Centre, PO Box 5050, Sudbury, Suffolk CO10 6ZQ.

DfEE *Supporting Pupils with Medical Needs.* Available free of charge from DfES Publications Centre, PO Box 5050, Sudbury, Suffolk CO10 6ZQ.

Organisations providing training in first aid:

British Red Cross Society, 9 Grosvenor Crescent, London, SW1X 7EJ.

St John Ambulance Association, 27 St John's Lane, Clerkenwell, London, EC1M 4BU.

St Andrew Ambulance Association, 48 Milton Street, Glasgow, G4 0HR.

Health and Safety

DfES (Department for Education and Skills) (2001) *Health and Safety: Responsibilities and Powers.* DfES 0803/2001.

HSC and HSE (Health and Safety Commissions and Executive). A wide range of publications on all aspects of health and safety available, most of them free of charge, from HSE Books, PO Box 1999, Sudbury, Suffolk, CO10 2WA.

The following are references or have particular relevance to safety and risk in schools.

HSC (1974) *Health and Safety at Work etc. Act.*

HSC (1999) *Management of Health and Safety at Work Regulations (+ Approved Code of Practice, L21).*

HSE (1990) *Handling of Loads* (EEC Directive 90/269).

HSE (1995) *Managing Health and Safety in Schools.*

HSE (1997) *First Aid Regulations.*

HSE (1997) *Reporting School Accidents,* Education Sheet No. 1.

HSE (1992; second edition 1998) *Health and Safety Guidance for School Governors and Members of School Boards.*

HSE (1999) RIDDOR *Everyone's Guide to the Reporting of Injuries, Diseases and Dangerous Occurrences Regulations.*

HSE (1998) *Five Steps to Risk Assessment.*

NPFA (National Playing Fields Association) 20 Ovington Square, London, SW3 1LQ. Advice and guidance on grounds, playgrounds and play apparatus.

ROSPA (Royal Society for the Prevention of Accidents) Edgbaston Park, 353 Bristol Road, Birmingham, B5 7SP. Advice as for NPFA above.

Sport and coaching

Sport England, 16 Upper Woburn House, London, WC1H 0QP. Information on all aspects of sport including addresses for all sports governing bodies and organisations with any link to sport.

Sports coach UK (formerly the National Coaching Foundation (NCF)) 114 Cardigan Road, Leeds, LS6 3BJ. Organises courses and publishes a wide variety of leaflets, books etc. on coaching. Many would be of real value to coaches and, in some instances, other AOTTs.

NCF *Code of Ethics and Conduct for Sports Coaches.*

NCF *Protecting Children: A Guide for Sportspeople.*

NCF *Safety and Injury.*

TOPS see Youth Sports Trust below.

Youth Sports Trust, Rutland Hall, Loughborough University, Loughborough, Leicestershire, LE11 3TU. The YST promotes the TOPS activity development programmes in primary schools (e.g. Top Sport and Top Play). Resource cards are provided which include points on safe practice. NB. The hockey NGB development programme at this age level is linked to TOPS. The badminton association point out that the practices and safety procedures they recommend are similar to those advocated in the TOPs programmes.

General bibliography and further reading

BAALPE, PEAUK, English Sports Council, NCF, *Guidelines for Local Education Authorities, Schools and Colleges in the use of ADULTS OTHER THAN TEACHERS in Physical Education and School Sport Programmes.*

Benn, T. and Benn, B. (1992) *Primary Gymnastics,* Cambridge: Cambridge University Press.

DfEE and QCA (2000) *Curriculum Guidance for the Foundation Stage.*

DfEE and QCA (1999) *National Curriculum for England: Physical Education.*

Dudley Advisory Services (1991) *Urban Adventure,* Dudley Education Services.

Dougherty, N.J., Auxter, D., Golberger, A.S., Heinzemanete, G.S. and Findlay, H.A. (1994) *Sport, Physical Activity and the Law,* Leeds: Human Kinetics.

Eve, N. (1994) 'Safety implications for partnerships – "in loco parentis"', *The Bulletin of Physical Education,* BAALPE, 30(3): 6–8.

Glover D.R. and Midura D.W. (1992) *Team Building Through Physical Challenges,* Leeds: Human Kinetics (on Outdoor and Adventurous Activities).

Gomberg, M. (1998) 'Teaching safely and teaching safety', *School Health and Safety Briefing,* Croner, 15: 1–4.

Harris, J. and Elbourn, J. (1997) *Teaching Health-Related Exercise at Key Stages 1 and 2,* Champaign, IL: Human Kinetics.

Hampshire County Council Education (1997) *Safety in Physical Education,* Education Department, The Castle, Winchester, SO23 8UG.

Hopper, B., Grey, J. and Maude, T. (2000) *Teaching Physical Education in the Primary School,* London: Routledge-Falmer.

Maude, P.M. (1997) *Primary Gymnastics,* London: Hodder and Stoughton.

Perkins, J. (1997) 'Safety issues for pupils with special educational needs in mainstream schools', *The Bulletin of Physical Education,* BAALPE, 33(3): 33–41.

Raymond, C. (1994) 'Legal awareness – some observations', *The Bulletin of Physical Education,* BAALPE, 30(2): 6–11.

Severs, J. (1991; third edition 1995) *Activities for PE Using Small Apparatus,* Cheltenham: Stanley Thornes.

Severs, J. (1994) *Striking and Fielding Games,* Hemel Hempstead: Simon and Schuster.

Suffolk County Council (1992) *Outdoor and Adventurous Activities at Key Stages One and Two,* Suffolk County Council Education Department.

Wetton, P. (1988) *Physical Education in the Nursery and Infant School,* London: Croom Helm.